Erwin Berry

The Alban Personnel Handbook for Congregations

An Alban Institute Publication

D1010184

Library of Congress Catalog Card Number 99-72204

ISBN 1-56699-214-1

CONTENTS

PREFACE

This handbook on personnel matters in a church setting is offered to assist your congregation in better managing its human resources. We are confident you will find the information and materials (including the policies, procedures, and forms in the appendix and on the CD-ROM) helpful in pursuing job performance excellence and commitment from your staff.

Even if your church uses the contents of this handbook in its entirety, however, each church will execute the plans, communicate the information, and apply the materials differently according to its unique situation. For that reason, the Alban Institute and the author are not responsible for the outcomes that result from the use of this handbook. We strongly recommend that you secure the services of an experienced, trained human resource professional to assist you in implementing the personnel system provided herein.

If an experienced human resource professional is not available in your church and you feel that you need assistance in implementing a new, comprehensive personnel system, my services can be secured on a consulting basis. I can be contacted at Organizational Development Strategies, Route 1, Box 750, Roseland, Virginia 22967; my phone number is (804) 325-7143. My services are not connected to the work of the Alban Institute and including this contact information here should neither imply that they endorse my consulting work nor that they are responsible for or guarantee its results.

One of the true mysteries to me, in my quest to gain a deeper understanding of how I might better serve Christ, is how and why we are placed in a particular place or situation at a particular point in time. As a Christian and Presbyterian, I believe each of us has a purpose in life; a reason for being. I, along with my wife, Joan, and our children, have been blessed to have known two pastors who have had profound impact on our lives. Dr. Bill Foster, who is now retired, inspired us during our early Christian "walk" while we were members of Trinity Presbyterian Church in Arlington, Virginia, where I first became an elder at age 24.

After retiring and relocating to Wintergreen Resort, Virginia, we had the good fortune to have Rev. Jim Wood as our pastor at First Presbyterian Church in Waynesboro (he is now pastor of First Presbyterian Church in Norfolk, Virginia). Jim is a man of many talents—some are God-given gifts, and others are skills that he has developed—as a visionary, an exemplary preacher, teacher, staff mentor and manager, and pastor. My faith has been strengthened for having served with him and his wife, Sheryl.

Jim spent 15 years as a company executive prior to entering the ministry. Because of that experience, he understands the importance of having policies, procedures, and systems in place to help a church accomplish its mission while serving the Lord. Shortly after Rev. Wood came to our church I remarked to some of my fellow officers that we would be lucky if we could keep him five years; it was our good fortune to have him as our pastor for four years. Now that Jim and his family have moved on to a larger congregation, I miss having him as my spiritual mentor as well as my friend!

The "Pastor's Perspectives on Theology and Ethics" in this book were written by Rev. Jim Wood. I am deeply grateful to him for writing those sections as well as for the guidance he gave me in developing a "user friendly" format for this handbook. His contributions surely make this a more useful resource for both pastors and lay leaders.

Why Your Church Needs a Personnel System

Over the past four decades I have had personnel-related experiences in four different churches: as an elder, as a deacon or an officer, and as a personnel liaison or personnel committee chair in both large and small Presbyterian and Baptist churches. Through these experiences, as well as through verbal exchanges with officers of other church denominations, I am convinced that churches of *all* denominations experience the same sorts of personnel-related problems. Hence, the reason for this personnel handbook.

The objective of this handbook is to provide both pastors and church lay leaders or officers with (1) a proven, comprehensive personnel system; (2) strategies to manage human resources and staff more effectively; and (3) an understanding of how to implement the processes needed to retain, motivate, and attract good personnel. This is not, however, a quick-fix approach to personnel management. The time period required to change or improve a church's (or any organization's) climate depends on multiple factors, including pastor-subordinate relationships; competitiveness and internal equity of salaries and benefits; job design (fairness of workload distribution); working conditions; and other personnel management practices that may be present when implementing the new personnel system. Therefore, only after your new personnel system has been in place for one to two years will your church notice an improved climate among its nonordained and ordained staff and officers. Moreover, you will gain an image in your community of being a good place to work.

Today's Employment Culture

Retaining and motivating your church's staff is important, especially in a time of low unemployment rates. Just as in business settings, congregations that experience high employee turnover convey to potential job applicants that unfavorable relations exist between the organization and its personnel. Once an employer has such a reputation or image in a community, it can take two to three years of demonstrating positive personnel practices to change that perception.

Since today's workforce is better educated (one-fourth have completed college), employees have higher expectations of their employers than was once the case. For instance, they want to participate in decisions that affect them and they want job advancement opportunities. They expect to receive equal pay for equal work (more of an issue for women than for men because, in general, women earn less than men for comparable jobs) as well as fair treatment in terms of working conditions, including personal leave to tend to family matters or illness. Also, today's employees tend to have less loyalty to an employer because of the recent history of organizational "downsizing" that resulted in less employee job security.

A Pastor's Perspective on Theology and Ethics

A quick look at a biblical concordance will not find the phrase "personnel policies and procedures" in any of the 27 New Testament books. What any study of the New Testament will find, however, are a plethora of references to structuring the body of Christ so that the Good News of Jesus Christ can be communicated most effectively. In the modern world of the church, this undoubtedly means efficient, effective, and fair staff relations. Paul's admonition to the Corinthian church that "all things be done decently and in order" (1 Corinthians 14:40)—although speaking of a particular issue related to that community's worship—is also a mandate to those who are in positions of responsibility within a congregation to establish a clearly defined and understood set of staff policies.

Melding the experience and expertise of the personnel business world with a strong commitment to the nurture and love present in the Christian gospel not only "greases the wheels" for smooth, efficient staff relationships, it also, in a very real way, models the gospel itself. First, it communicates that we care enough for the staff and the congregation to set these policies in place. Second, it shows that we care enough about the calling of the church to model our relationships on those presented to us in Scripture.

This handbook sets forth the basics of enacting such a biblical mandate to nurture its staff (arguably its most valuable asset) through a clearly outlined set of policies and procedures. While intensely practical, it takes seriously the theological and ethical issues that should undergird everything that takes place in the church.

People of faith all agree on our responsibility to nurture each other. Just as Scripture is valuable to provide a map for ordering our personal lives, so is it valuable for the church as well. We need to set forth clear staff policies. Letting each staff member know what is expected and how she or he will be evaluated not only makes sense but also is firmly founded on the model of the New Testament.

Why then do we so often do it so poorly? Too often, it is because we don't have the tools. Well, here are the tools.

How to Use This Book

The Alban Personnel Handbook for Congregations is designed to give church leaders the information and tools they need to implement an effective personnel system in their church. It is divided into two parts: (1) the text, which is made up of chapters that examine the different elements of the system, and (2) the appendixes, which reproduce the policies and procedures, forms, and samples referred to in the text. The appendixes are also included on the CD-ROM so that they can be adapted as necessary for use in your church. For more information on using the appendixes and the CD-ROM, refer to the information at the beginning of the appendix section.

Each chapter begins with a narrative that poses a hypothetical personnel situation to introduce the topic(s) covered within that chapter. These narratives, set at what I call Stone Church, a fictional parish of indeterminate denominational affiliation, are all based on situations that I have actually experienced as a church officer and personnel liaison and personnel committee chair.

CHAPTER 1

Getting Started: Assessing Your Situation

The Situation at Stone Church

Stone Church, founded in 1899, is located in a town of 20,000 in the south-eastern United States that has experienced 5 percent population growth in the past three years. There are 300 members on the church roll, which is down 5 percent in the past three years and 15 percent in the past 15 years. Forty percent of those members are over 50 years old. Stone Church has an annual budget of $200,000, which is down 7 percent in the past three years.

Bruce, pastor of Stone Church, was installed three years ago; this is the second church he has served since graduating from seminary. Stone has twice the membership and annual budget of his previous church. Stone Church's previous pastor had served there for 10 years prior to Bruce's installation.

Stone's nonordained staff members are all part-time employees except Jean, who has been the full-time secretary for the past 12 years. She is married to Chuck, who has been Stone's Director of Christian Education (DCE) for 17 years and also teaches at the local high school. The other staff members were all hired recently after three longtime employees left within a year. Marjorie has been choir director and organist for three months; she replaced Elizabeth, who moved away suddenly to take another job after 12 years of service. Brenda has been bookkeeper for six months, replacing an employee of 14 years. Seth, the janitor/housekeeper replaced a 15-year employee one year ago.

Stone's only written personnel policies are in the form of church memoranda and personnel committee minutes. Until this year the personnel committee had not had a single member (including the chair) who had human resource experience and training. Ned, the current personnel liaison, is the human resource director for the local branch of a national corporation. Bruce's predecessor met with the personnel committee only once a year when salary awards were determined for himself and the staff. Also, Bruce did not have a formal personnel system at the first church he served as pastor.

Bruce inherited an unfavorable employee work climate that has culminated in excessive employee turnover. Overlapping job duties have resulted in a haphazard distribution of work. Other problems include inequities in salaries paid and benefits provided, poor office workstation arrangement, and antiquated office equipment, including no personal computers. Complicating these problems are a lack of church and staff goals; the absence of a performance evaluation process; and communication difficulties that result in misunderstandings and rumors among the staff, officers, and congregation. Needless to say, there is considerable unrest among the staff and officers! Bruce recognizes the need for a personnel system.

Ned has just completed an assessment of Stone's current personnel policies and practices, which he has given to Bruce and the church officers. He has scheduled a meeting the next week to discuss the assessment findings and recommendations with Bruce and the officers.

A Pastor's Perspective on Theology and Ethics

We hear so often the comment that the pastor has too much control, but in my experience, most pastors are not power-hungry folk who are intent on wresting all control away from the congregation. What happens is that, too often, pastors are pushed into making what appear to be unilateral decisions because the lay leadership is not prepared to share in the responsibilities of leadership. No place does this have the potential to create more of a rub in the church than in its personnel practices.

Whether it be how a pastor prioritizes the duties that are part of her or his call or the way the staff reports to each other and the congregation, I have come to realize that most of the potential problems are built into the system, or, more accurately, happen by default until someone decides to complain—usually too late. This is where a set of clearly defined policies can literally be a godsend. Personnel policies should never be at the whim of a pastor or a governing board. They should be guided by a clearly defined structure and accompanying procedures.

The Organization Development Process: An Overview

This handbook provides you with an organization development approach to managing your church's human, physical, and financial resources more effectively and also offers a fresh, alternative committee structure for man-

2

aging the programs and activities of your church. Organization development focuses on ensuring that facility, financial, human resource, and church member needs are well balanced. The organization development approach also deals with planning for orderly and cost-effective church growth while providing staff the opportunity to participate in developing church and personal goals and to realize financial reward for their contributions toward those goals.

The pastor and officers should develop together an annual *strategic plan* for the church that will serve as a "road map" for accomplishing its *goals,* which should relate directly to its *mission statement.* These terms are defined as follows:

- *Strategic Plan.* A strategic plan is a written document (sometimes referred to as a business plan) prepared by the ordained and nonordained staff and church officers that covers a two- to five-year period and focuses on those activities that will maximize service to God while minimizing congregational risks and resistance. If you do not currently have such a plan in place, start with a one-year strategic plan before moving on to longer plans.
- *Goals.* Goals are written statements that are measurable qualitatively and quantitatively and that directly relate to your church's strategic plan. The staff, officers, and church committees should all develop annual goals.
- *Mission Statement.* A church's mission statement incorporates the goals of your church, the broader goals of your denomination, and the ultimate goal of better serving Christ.

Personnel Policy and System Assessment

Your existing personnel processes and staffing structure must be considered when you determine how best to integrate a new system with your old system in order to minimize the resistance from your staff, officers, and congregation. In most congregations, the senior pastor is ultimately responsible for the personnel function and its administration. Moreover, most churches, regardless of membership size, have an entity (usually a committee) responsible for addressing staff personnel matters. In turn, this committee undoubtedly has a chairperson who may or may not be an officer of your church.

To begin your process of developing a new personnel management system, the lay leader or officer responsible for personnel matters (ideally

3

a trained human resource professional) should undertake a formal assessment of current nonordained staff personnel policies, procedures, and practices. This includes the compensation and benefit plan you offer them. The salary and benefit (compensation) policy for ordained staff should also be assessed if your denomination does not have a mandatory compensation plan. When you investigate your denomination's benefit plan coverage and/ or compare its cost with other denominational plans, you are likely to discover that your church can lower the cost and/or increase the benefits of your current plan (see chapter 5).

The assessment findings should then be organized into categories, under the headings of personnel policies, procedures, and practices (see pages 6–7 for a list of possible categories). The personnel committee chair/ officer should then prepare specific recommendations on how to integrate the current personnel practices into the system described in this handbook. (see How to Integrate the Old Personnel System into the New on page 57 for an in-depth description of the procedure). I recommend that the personnel committee chair give a copy of the assessment report to the pastor and church officers for review prior to orally presenting the report to them.

The senior pastor should also conduct an assessment of personnel functions and policies. I recommend this five-step process:

1. *Observe* how the church functions for at least six months prior to instituting any changes except those that are essential;
2. *Review* written personnel policies, procedures, and practices;
3. *Meet* personally with the chair of the personnel committee;
4. *Attend* the personnel committee meeting; and
5. *Identify* potential committee members, even though it will not be possible to make changes to staffing committees (personnel and others) immediately.

When recruitment of members for various committees is ready to begin, allow the pastor to have input before final selections are made. Conscious consideration should be made to recruit some committee members who have the capacity to become committee chairs. An effective strategy for a three-year committee rotation is to select members in their second year on a committee to act as a vice-chair who would become the chair in their third year of service. Ideally, the personnel committee is made up of at least three or four church officers and three or four members from the congregation at large. A church is only as strong as its committee members, officers, and staff.

Personnel Policy and Procedures Manual

The foundation for an effective personnel system is to have written personnel policies and procedures in a manual that is reviewed and updated on an annual basis.

- *Policy.* A policy is a written statement that defines a church's position with respect to broad directives that church officers and the pastor have approved. These policies, when formally monitored and evaluated, ensure that long-term church goals are accomplished in a consistent and orderly manner by the pastor, officers, and church staff. Personnel policy statements may be written by a church officer and then referred to the pastor and the personnel liaison or personnel committee chair (as explained in chapter 2, I prefer a church organization structure that identifies one person as responsible for personnel matters—the personnel liaison—rather than a committee and its chair). Together, they will determine if the recommended policy is needed (see Policy and Procedure Development, Policy 100.0, on page 61).
- *Procedure.* A procedure is a written explanation of how a policy is executed. (The appendixes to this handbook contain the essential personnel policies and procedures necessary for effective management of your church's personnel practices.) In order to create a positive climate of trust within your faith community and between the pastor, staff, and officers, it is essential that your employees be treated fairly and consistently with regard to personnel matters (see Personnel Philosophy, Policy 600.0, on page 63).

As important as gaining the church officers' approval of personnel policies and procedures is the education process that must ensue after such approval is obtained. I recommend the following process:

1. The personnel liaison or personnel committee chair distributes copies of the policy and procedure manual to the pastor, secretary, and committee chairs. The bookkeeper gets the Personnel Action Notice and payroll record-keeping information only, while other staff have access to the manual retained by the Secretary.
2. The personnel liaison or personnel committee chair then conducts a briefing session to familiarize these persons with the personnel policies, procedures, and forms.
3. The personnel liaison or personnel committee chair meets with the church's steering committee, which I call the Focus and Direction Task

5

Force (F & D) (see chapter 2), regarding two important components of the system: performance evaluations for the pastor and other ordained staff (a process described in chapter 5) and surveys of committee members and church officers designed to measure the effectiveness of the church's operations (see chapter 6).

4. At least every two years, F & D should review all church policies and procedures to ensure that they are still applicable and to determine if any new policies or procedures are needed. The F & D member who identifies the need for a new or revised policy or procedure then submits a draft of the proposed policy or procedure to the pastor for his or her input. If a policy or procedure is personnel related, the personnel liaison or personnel committee chair should also receive a copy of the proposed policy change draft (see Policy and Procedure Development, Policy 100.0, on page 61).

A key ingredient in building a church in both quality and quantity is the development of annual goals or objectives for each committee, as well as for the pastor and staff (a process explored in chapter 4).

The following list of personnel policies, procedures, and forms will help you organize the materials discussed in this handbook (all of the materials are reproduced in the appendixes):

PERSONNEL POLICIES, PROCEDURES, AND PRACTICES	SYNOPSIS AND USE
Employee Classifications Overview (page 58)	Contains guidelines for distinguishing among ordained and nonordained, salaried and hourly, and full-time and part-time positions.
Policy and Procedure Development Policy (page 61)	Defines policy and establishes a system for its execution, preparation, approval, and control.
Personnel Philosophy Policy (page 63)	Conveys the church's commitment to build trust with its employees.
Employment Policy (page 64)	Contains policies for how the church will create new positions, determine pay ranges, handle substance abuse or sexual harassment, and administer its benefit and retirement plans and procedures for how it will hire employees and note changes in employee status.

PERSONNEL POLICIES, PROCEDURES, AND PRACTICES	SYNOPSIS AND USE
Employment Forms and Samples (pages 67–77)	Forms that are required to be used by personnel policy: job description, employment application, employment application supplement for salaried nonordained staff, employment reference investigation, employment reference inquiry, employment offer letter sample, federal immigration form, employee orientation procedure and checklist, personnel action notice, and job performance goals.
Employee Fair Treatment Policy (page 78)	Policy and procedure for employees to follow when they feel they have not been treated fairly.
Employee Discipline Policy (page 79)	Explains how discipline for substandard job performance or a policy violation is administered.
Employee Leave of Absence Policy (page 83)	Identifies the types of approved absences, how wages and benefits are affected, and how leaves are initiated.
Salary and Performance Evaluation Administration Policy (page 86)	Outlines the process by which employees' pay and performance are reviewed; defines levels of performance and procedures for communicating with employee about performance.
Performance Evaluation and Improvement Plan Forms (page 91–96)	Forms for use in performance evaluations; one for nonordained staff, one for ordained staff, and one for salaried nonordained and ordained staff focusing on goals.
Employee Exit Interview Policy (page 97)	Explains how to conduct an exit interview and how to report on its results.
Working Conditions of Salaried Staff Policy (page 98)	Ensures that ordained staff are covered by policies that give them adequate time off.
Annual Officer Survey of Service Experience Form (page 99)	Form that can be used to evaluate effectiveness, satisfaction, and working relationships of church officers.

7

PERSONNEL POLICIES, PROCEDURES, AND PRACTICES	SYNOPSIS AND USE
Annual Committee Survey of Service Experience Form (page 100)	Form that can be used to evaluate effectiveness, satisfaction, and working relationships of committee members.
Employee Handbook (page 101)	Distributed to all employees, summarizing policies and outlining what they can expect from the church and what the church expects from them.

CHAPTER 2

Enhancing Your Present Personnel System: Church Organization and Job Structure

Pastor Bruce has been frustrated with most of Stone Church's committees because they lack a sense of urgency in addressing business matters. Nor do they have any strategies in place to rebuild the membership, which has been declining for several years. The present committee structure has been in place for as long as anyone can remember.

Bruce has called a meeting with Ned, the personnel liaison, who, as a senior church officer, has shown himself to be someone who always gets the tasks that are assigned to him done in a timely, cost-effective manner. Prior to their conference, Ned received a note from Bruce asking him to think about how the committees could be made more effective. They agreed to meet at the church to discuss the matter at a mutually convenient time.

At their conference Ned suggested that the nominating committee chair and Bruce needed to identify persons from the church who have leadership potential as future officers and could serve in at-large positions on committees. To start this process, Ned gave Bruce a list of current officers in their first year of service and the names of congregation members he felt had the capacity and inclination to become at-large committee persons. Bruce then presented to Ned a "fresh" approach for restructuring church committees.

A Pastor's Perspective on Theology and Ethics

Although Christian traditions disagree on the meaning of the word *bishop* in Paul's first letter to Timothy (1 Timothy 3:1-7) or whether the qualifications for a deacon need to be reinterpreted in light of modern world circumstances (1 Timothy 3:8-13), what can be agreed upon is that the early Christians had a structure for staffing the church. This pattern has changed over the centuries in the institutional church. What has not changed, however, is the need for the church to delineate clearly areas of responsibility and structure for its staffing.

From the sixth chapter of Acts we can see that the earliest church recognized the need to delegate responsibilities, which resulted in the calling of the first deacons. Just as the early church found that the twelve apostles could not do it all, so our congregations need to know that, regardless of the size of the congregation, no one person can do it all.

We can also learn from Scripture that the best way to nurture our church leaders is by setting clean boundaries, clearly articulating duties, and outlining reasonable expectations for all employees. This might sound like simple common sense; yet it is amazing how few congregations set out clear job descriptions and rarely, if ever, provide for an effective job performance evaluation or review process.

Organization Structure

A segment of the organization assessment report should contain the church's staff organization chart, which shows reporting relationships and authority. The following examples show how Stone Church is currently organized and its proposed new structure:

Stone Church's Current Organization Chart

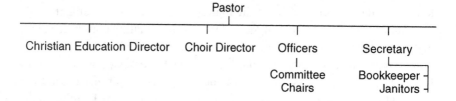

Stone Church's Proposed Organization Chart

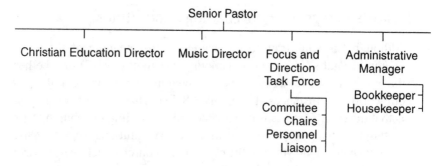

Church Personnel Roles

- **Senior Pastor:** The spiritual leadership of the congregation and management of the church staff is the primary responsibility of the pastor, with support from the church staff. For larger churches, the role of an associate pastor should be identified on the organization chart (e.g., congregational care, youth ministry, etc.).
- **Focus and Direction Task Force (F & D) or Church Officers:** Their function is to focus on church polity and strategic matters and to direct actions that will accomplish church goals, as well as personnel and other goals. I have found that a Focus and Direction Task Force is effective because it not only facilitates the church accomplishing its goals but also reduces the number of lay governing bodies and committees with which the pastor must be personally involved. (For more information about F & D, see Committee Structure Model later in this chapter.)
- **Personnel Liaison or Personnel Committee Chair:** This person has primary responsibility for overseeing all personnel-related matters as directed by F & D, including personnel policy and procedure implementation and education.
- **Secretary or Administrative Manager:** She or he is responsible for coordinating all personnel-related actions for the church and the senior pastor, as approved by F & D, and maintains employee files.

Committee Structure Model

In my experience, more is not necessarily better, especially with regard to the number of committees and the number of members on each committee. Remember, a pastor has only so many hours each day or week to devote to attending committee meetings, so the number of committees has a direct impact on the pastor's time allocations and commitments. (Later in this chapter I will introduce a policy that will help the pastor and other ordained staff balance their time commitments to church, family, community, and personal pursuits.)

There are many different structural models for you to consider. Based on my own experience, I recommend that you look at adopting an organization structure comprised of a five committee system coupled with a Focus and Direction Task Force (F & D). The model I recommend consists of the following committees and their respective responsibilities (though I have listed subcommittees only under the administration committee, any of the committees may choose to form subcommittees for specific functions):

- **Worship:** Responsible for the worship service, music, communion, and so forth;
- **Mission:** Organizes and draws attention to local, area, and worldwide involvements and events;
- **Community Outreach:** Focuses on church and community outreach programs and activities;
- **Education:** Has responsibility for Christian education (of both children and adults) and any preschool/graded school programs located in the church;
- **Administration:** This should consist of a personnel liaison or personnel subcommittee (to handle nonordained and ordained staff personnel matters), a property and maintenance subcommittee, and a stewardship subcommittee (each having a coordinator). The chair of this committee develops the annual budget along with the entire administration committee.
- **Focus and Direction Task Force (F & D).** This group functions as an officer steering committee and is comprised of the chairs of the five committees listed above, the pastor (who serves as moderator), the personnel liaison, and the church secretary. Remember, the more involved the secretary or administrative manager is in church polity matters, the better able she or he is to serve as an emissary and "barometer" of church member attitudes for the pastor. Ideally, F & D meets at the beginning of a church year, after the committee chairs are selected, to formulate goals for the coming year and thereafter on an "as needed" basis (but at least quarterly).

To develop a collegial climate among the church staff and officers, consider holding annual or semiannual weekend retreats where the officers along with the ordained and nonordained staff can plan, solve problems, worship, and engage in recreation together. This is a wonderful way for the pastor and staff to outline their vision, propose goals for the new year, and present those accepted goals to the officers so that they can finalize the church's strategic plan. Follow-up meetings at the church may be necessary to refine those goals and formulate the plan. (Chapter 7 has more information on organizing staff/officer retreats.)

The Personnel Liaison

An alternative to having a personnel committee (or subcommittee) for handling personnel-related matters is for the pastor and nominating committee chair to identify one person to serve as the personnel liaison of the administration committee. The personnel liaison should ideally be a trained human resource professional and/or a church officer who has served on a personnel committee previously. Just as important, she or he should be sensitive to personnel matters and someone who can be a "sounding board" for the pastor regarding potential personnel actions.

The personnel liaison is responsible for educating the pastor, secretary or administrative manager, and the committee chairs (each year as chairpersons change) on personnel-related matters. In addition to having primary responsibility for overseeing all personnel-related actions, the personnel liaison should serve on all search committees for staff positions. Such involvement will ensure that personnel policy and procedures are followed.

My own experience in such a position has been instructive. In one church where I served as personnel liaison but was not required by policy to serve on all search committees, I was involved in a situation where the chair of a search committee did not follow established personnel policy and procedures regarding the recruitment of a music director. Not until after they offered the position to the candidate did they (1) obtain a completed employment application form from that person; (2) investigate employment references; and (3) use the employment offer letter for the person they selected (these steps are detailed in chapter 3).

Luckily, when I got involved and had the search committee chair complete the required employment policy and procedures, the individual's references were checked and found to be excellent. The search committee chair, however, had told the music director, by now on the job, that she would be covered by health insurance from "day one" instead of after the three-month training period required by policy. Although the situation was eventually ironed out, all involved found themselves in an awkward position regarding employment practices that could have been avoided if the personnel liaison had been part of the search process from the beginning.

If you adopt the personnel liaison organization structure, it is imperative that the pastor notify the personnel liaison prior to initiating any personnel action (for instance, staff recruitment, wage increases, disciplinary actions, and so forth) to ensure that personnel policies and procedures are followed. The intermediary between the personnel liaison or the chair of the personnel committee and the pastor in charge of personnel matters is traditionally the church secretary or administrative manager, who also serves as the personnel coordinator.

Assessing a Church's Personnel System

As mentioned in chapter 1, if your church has a personnel system in place, it is wise to have the personnel liaison or personnel committee chair assess the effectiveness of your personnel policies, procedures, and practices at least every other year. If your church does not have a personnel system, select an officer—preferably someone with training as a human resource professional—to undertake a formal assessment of the personnel practices presently employed. A good starting place for the person conducting the assessment is to speak with the church secretary, who usually carries out most of the personnel actions pertaining to staff employment, such as pay, benefits, vacation, and so forth.

Job Design and Descriptions

Two key parts of assessing your personnel system are to evaluate your job descriptions and to understand the job classifications you use. The first step in the development of job descriptions for each staff position, ordained and nonordained, is to examine the design of each job by writing out a list of job tasks in the order in which they should be performed (see the Sample Job Description on page 67). Chapter 4 relates the job description to a performance goals evaluation system.

A job description identifies to whom a position reports directly (for instance, the pastor) and indirectly (for instance, the worship committee); it also may list minimum qualifications required to perform a position. An organization chart (as shown on page 10) reveals reporting relationships and authority.

Job Classification System

The guidelines that follow are not intended to make you an expert regarding job classifications but rather to give you a better understanding of the rationale for and application of such a system. One important aspect of a personnel system is to have a policy that states that the personnel liaison or personnel committee is responsible for administering the job classification system. A job classification system also provides a basis for developing salary ranges (which are addressed in chapter 5). Jobs should be broken down into ordained and nonordained, salaried and hourly, and full-time and part-time position classifications. The following are important variables that need to be taken into account when classifications are devised:

- **Ordained and Nonordained Church Positions:** These jobs, including preschool personnel, are exempt from federal and state labor laws.
- **Church Graded School Positions:** These personnel (grades one and higher) are subject to federal labor laws. State labor laws vary from state to state, but generally classify positions such as graded school directors and teachers as "exempt" (exempt from overtime pay requirements) and may be salaried. Teacher aides and helpers would generally be classified as "nonexempt" (not exempt from overtime pay requirements) and paid on an hourly wage basis.
- **Overtime Pay:** Nonexempt employees who work more than 40 hours per week must be paid one and one-half times their base wage for any hours worked in excess of 40 hours. Failure to pay a nonexempt employee for all the hours worked constitutes a violation of federal and state wage and hour laws, punishable by a fine and the payment of back wages to the complaining employee. A federal and/or state wage and hour compliance officer can scrutinize past pay records as far back as the complaining employee feels she or he has not been paid appropriately (payment could be retroactive to an employee's date of employment).
- **Reporting Time Worked:** The bookkeeper, secretary, or other person handling payroll matters should establish a procedure for nonexempt employees to record their actual hours worked each day and for each pay period (weekly, biweekly, semimonthly, or monthly). Time worked in excess of 40 hours may not be carried forward to the next work week but must be paid at the overtime rate. The simplest procedure is to have the payroll coordinator issue time cards to these employees which they are responsible for turning in at the end of each pay period so paychecks can be produced according to the actual hours worked. Time cards can be purchased at most office supply stores. Keeping accurate records of employee hours worked and paid as well as vacation, sick, and family leave time taken and paid is critical for your church. Labor laws also require that nonexempt employees be paid for

training and meetings if attendance is mandatory and the function is directly related to the employee's job.

- **Payroll Records:** You are required by federal law to keep payroll records for three years.
- **Minimum Wage:** Effective September 1, 1997, the federal minimum wage was established at $5.15 per hour. Federal law exempts churches from paying the minimum wage to their employees but, for the sake of offering a fair wage, I recommend that you pay at least the federal minimum wage for an entry-level position.
- **Full-Time Status:** If you have not defined in writing (or in practice) what constitutes a "full-time" employee, I suggest that you adopt a policy stating that an employee who works at least 35 hours per week for at least six months per year be classified as "full time."
- **Part-Time Status:** Likewise, if you have no other written policy in place, I suggest that you adopt a policy stating that an employee who works less than 35 hours per week or less than six months per year be classified as "part time."
- **Work Policy for Ordained Staff:** Even though a pastor and other ordained staff are exempt from overtime pay regardless of the number of hours they work, it is essential that your church control the hours per week they are expected to work by distributing to the officers and congregation a written policy covering this important matter. As you realize, during the day pastors normally keep office hours, visit members at the hospital and at home, conduct funerals, and attend church, denominational, and other job-related meetings. In addition, pastors and other ordained staff often attend church meetings at night, officiate at marriages on Saturdays, and conduct worship services on Sundays. In my opinion, no more than 50 hours week for the pastor and other ordained staff is reasonable, with two days (preferably consecutive) identified as their scheduled days off (see Working Conditions of Salaried Staff, Policy 607.0, on page 98).

CHAPTER 3

Avoiding Staffing Problems: The Employee Search, Employment, and Training Process

Bruce got the message on his voice mail: Elizabeth, Stone Church's choir director and accompanist, was moving across the country. She had been so nervous about telling the church that she held off until the last possible moment; she would be gone in two weeks.

When Bruce went to the personnel committee with the bad news, they were as lost as he was. Comments and questions bounced around the room: "What are we going to do?" "We only have two weeks before she goes; we have to solve this immediately!" "This is a crucial time in this church's life, if we have to go without music, it could have long-term effects on our congregation's health." The meeting went downhill from there.

After the all-too-usual "sackcloth and ashes," they finally decided that a group of members from the choir serve as the search committee for the new position. Bruce was told to ask for volunteers from the choir at their next rehearsal: "Volunteers make the best committee members" was the comment that won the day. They all figured that if the choir had to work with the person, the choir should make the decision. Bruce was to keep a "healthy distance" from the process. While he had gotten along well enough with Elizabeth, he had a few issues with the direction—or lack thereof—of the music program. The group therefore decided that he should not be involved with the employment process and let the choir determine what it wanted in its director.

The search committee fell into place rather easily and a classified advertisement ran the next week in the local newspaper. The ad asked applicants to submit a resume and written employment references. One week later, two resumes had been received and, on the strength of those credentials, Marjorie was hired. She met Bruce only after the committee had offered her the position. Since there were so few applicants and little time to spare, Marjorie never filled out an employment application form and no one ever checked out her employment references. "After all, beggars can't be choosers," one of the search committee members said.

One year later, Bruce found himself in the uncomfortable position of knowing that Marjorie was not working out as an employee. It had been downhill almost from the very beginning, with increasing dissension, lost choir members, frustration from the congregation, and a lot of hair-pulling on Bruce's part.

The old adage that "hindsight is 20/20" didn't mean much in this situation. "After all, what could I have done differently?" he thought to himself. Elizabeth had left with only two weeks notice when her husband relocated. "A church needs music, doesn't it? There wasn't anyone in the congregation who could fill in, was there? We had to fill the vacancy quickly." Marjorie's resume neither suggested that she had been let go from more than one previous position nor that she lacked the talents that matched the needs of the congregation. The comment that "beggars can't be choosers" filled his cranium like a bad head cold.

How to Avoid Staffing Problems

Anyone who has been a part of a congregation long enough has probably caught Bruce's head cold at one time or another. Hindsight might highlight the problem, but the key to effective leadership is not to let history repeat itself.

All employment problems bring pain and division, especially if they lead to termination; it is a fact of life. If left unaddressed, these problems can cause damage to the congregation that takes years to heal. Most problems, however, can be prevented from the beginning. It might sound trite and elementary, but hiring the right person for a position is essential. What could Bruce and the personnel committee have done to ensure that they employed the right person?

How can you avoid serious problems with church employees and hire the right people? The secrets are to (1) never rush an employment process; (2) stay calm, even when you feel under pressure or in a bind; (3) openly communicate with your congregation (ask for patience!); and (4) implement the proven employment process that I outline below. (Performance evaluation and employee warning procedures designed to aid a supervisor in helping an employee correct job-related deficiencies, also important to preventing problems, are discussed in chapter 5.).

In the case of Stone Church, they did not have an effective employment process in place when Marjorie was hired. Consider these mistakes:

The search committee was made up only of choir members; applicants for advertised position openings submitted only resumes and did not complete employment application forms; a search committee member did not investigate employment references by phone; retail credit and criminal reports were not obtained for applicant finalists; the pastor was not involved in the interview process; and no personnel liaison or member of the personnel committee was on the search committee.

Employment of Staff Personnel

Employment of church staff generally falls into two categories: unplanned staff replacement and planned additions to staff. The general processes for hiring these positions is similar, but they differ in how monies are allocated to fund the positions.

With unplanned staff replacements (as with Stone Church's choir director), money should already be in the budget for the person to be replaced. Therefore, special financial authorization or allocation should not be necessary except approval by lay officers of expenditure involved in replacing the position.

Making a planned addition to your staff will grow more organically out of your personnel assessment process. At the time you are preparing the annual budget for next year (usually in the early fall, assuming your budget is based on a calendar year), the committee or individual who is responsible for budget development, along with the pastor and the Focus and Direction Task Force, should determine if any additions or deletions to the staff should be made. Once the appropriate approvals are obtained, use the same search process for both situations presented below.

Staff Search Committee Formation

Having strict selection criteria for the search committee members will facilitate employing a qualified individual. The pastor or the supervisor of the person who directly supervises the position and the committee chair or lay officer to which the position indirectly reports should select congregational members at large to serve on a search committee. From my experience, the ideal search committee is made up of eight members: one officer (for instance, the worship committee chair for a music director search); five church members (for instance, for the choir director search you might ask two adult choir members, preferably including one with formal music education or work experience, a children's music coordinator, and two at-large congregational members); the personnel liaison or a personnel committee member; and, in an ex-officio position, the pastor or other ordained staff person responsible for the position.

The search committee chair should be selected from those members who agree to serve on the committee. The committee chair should be a "doer," one who has demonstrated the ability to organize, direct, and communicate effectively, who will initiate the search in a timely manner, and who is personally committed to the search. I recommend you use a search committee to fill every position, regardless of level or pay.

Communication with the Congregation

The search committee chair should announce to your membership the position you are recruiting. Get the information out as soon as possible, using the church newsletter, a bulletin board posting, and/or a special mailing. Include in your announcement the job description, the minimal qualifications needed by applicants, and names of committee members to be contacted with referrals, since members of your church may be able to recommend candidates.

Keep your congregation informed at least monthly of your search progress. When the position has been filled, the search committee chair should inform the congregation of the new employee's name, qualifications, starting date, and salary. (The importance of having salary ranges in place that are based on current salary/benefit survey data, which will enable you to offer a competitive and fair wage for your job opening, is addressed in chapter 5).

Employee Recruitment

Your ability to select qualified employees who are capable of meeting your church's program goals is predicated upon the employment process you have in place, the make-up of the search committee, and having a current job description (see the discussion of job descriptions in chapter 2).

The appendix and the CD-ROM contain all the employment forms you need for initiating your search. You should, however, appoint one member of the search committee, preferably one of the lay members, to write a one-page statement about your church, including the name and address of your church; a contact person with work and home phone numbers; membership size; the annual budget with specific figures relevant to the position;

community size and location; biographical sketches of the pastor and other ordained staff as applicable; other job-relevant information; and a cut-off date for receiving resumes and employment applications.

Indicate the salary you can offer by using the phrase, "salary commensurate with experience and education" (such a strategy will enable you to attract applicants for salaried positions who might not respond if you advertised a salary range that is under a prospective applicant's present salary). Also indicate the benefits offered and what moving expense reimbursement is available, if applicable. Such statements are particularly helpful in listing openings for church musicians with music guilds, colleges with respected music departments, and other musical institutions.

Be creative in your search. Make direct contacts with persons at other churches in your area that have strong staffing reputations; they may know of or could be candidates themselves. In addition, there may be persons in your area who recently retired from fields related to the position for which you are hiring, and they may well be interested in continuing to work. Advertise your opening in other churches' newsletters and/or post notices on their most conspicuous church bulletin boards. Again, church members may know of a candidate for your position opening.

Advertising

If your search committee has a human resource professional as a member, which is ideal, such a person could personally handle the technical aspects of a search, including writing and placing advertisements. As mentioned, direct contacts are generally more productive, but newspapers can also be effective. Where and when you place an advertisement is all-important in reaching candidates for a job opening, since there are only a handful of appropriate candidates available for most church positions.

Since you have not budgeted for expenses related to unplanned staff replacements, you need to get the most "bang for your buck" by running your advertisements on the days when most people read the paper. Generally, you will get greater response to advertisements run in the Sunday papers. Wednesday, when grocery specials and coupons appear, is the next best day of the week to run employment ads. Don't be lured into buying a "package" of multiple insertion ads by a newspaper salesperson. It is more cost effective to be selective in your placement of advertisements. If you currently have an announcement regarding Sunday worship services and other church activities (usually in the Saturday edition of your local newspaper), running a display advertisement on the same page where your announcement appears could prove fruitful.

Types of Newspaper Advertisements

- **Display:** For professional or salaried positions, when you know there will be a limited number of potential candidates (especially positions like music director or youth director that require specialized education or experience), your best advertising strategy is to spend your money on display ads. Display advertisements generally appeal to individuals who aren't necessarily looking for a new position. The lead time for a display advertisement is no less than seven days prior to the day of publication.
- **Classified Display:** Most newspapers offer classified display ads, which are similar in layout to a display ad but are located at the beginning of the classified advertising section. Such ads can be used for most positions, sometimes in combination with a display advertisement.
- **Classified:** These are usually used for nonprofessional or hourly wage positions.

Preparing Effective Advertisements

The key ingredients of an effective advertisement are (1) the newspapers in which you place your ad, (2) the day(s) of week the ad will appear, (3) the wording and presentation of your ad, and (4) the number of insertions.

- **Step 1—Selecting Newspaper(s):** Identify cities and their newspapers within your church's immediate area.
- **Step 2—Type of Advertisement:** Phone or visit your local newspaper and ask to speak with a salesperson in the advertising department about the sort of ad (display, classified display, or classified) you feel will best appeal to applicants for your job opening. Your advertising sales representative can assist you in preparing your ad's layout.
- **Step 3—Layout:** As illustrated below, I have found that an advertisement for professional positions approximately two column inches high by two column inches wide with a heavy black border and the job title in large, bold capital letters improves readership and applicant response:

```
┌─────────────────────────────────────────┐
│              MUSIC DIRECTOR               │
│                                           │
│  Stone Church has an immediate opening for│
│  an individual with at least five years   │
│  experi-                                  │
│  ence directing adult and youth choirs.   │
│  Position does not require accompaniment of│
│  choirs but organ/piano playing ability   │
│  desirable. Send resume with experience,  │
│  education and present salary to: Erwin   │
│  Berry,                                   │
│  Chair, Search Committee, Stone Church,   │
│  Box 1, Stone, ST 00000                   │
└─────────────────────────────────────────┘
```

- **Step 4—Placement:** If you are placing a display advertisement, request that the ad be located on the first page of the paper's appropriate section for greatest visibility.
- **Step 5—Frequency:** Run your display ad on a week-by-week basis. After running your ad the first time, the newspaper will probably require three to four days lead time to rerun your ad. I suggest that you budget for running your advertisements at least four successive weeks (Sundays and Wednesdays plus the religion section, often Saturday) in at least two different newspapers.

Legal and Ethical Issues

In today's employment environment, I believe that job applicants have more rights under our judicial system than does an employer. Employers are restricted as to the information they can solicit from a job applicant due to the Civil Rights Act referred to below. The Equal Employment Opportunity Commission (EEOC) and the Department of Labor and Justice Department are charged with enforcing this federal law.

Therefore, before discussing employment screening and interviews, some legal and ethical issues must be considered. Your entire search process, from advertising to interviewing to final selection must be conducted in a way that will avoid discrimination problems. This poses challenging questions that need careful consideration. For instance, if your church staff is made up of all men, can you advertise for a woman for the sake of gender balance? If your church is Presbyterian, can you advertise for a music director who is Presbyterian, since she or he would be more familiar with the music of your denomination? No, you cannot. It would be considered discriminatory to advertise for applicants specifying a particular gender or church affiliation. However, if a member of your church or

23

denomination applies for an advertised position, is found to be the best qualified applicant, and is ultimately hired, it would not be considered discriminatory. In the same way, if you find a female candidate to be the best qualified and you ultimately hire a woman, it also would not be considered discriminatory (see information below on relevant federal and state laws).

Federal and State Laws

The federal laws discussed below apply to all states. Please note, however, that since employment laws vary from state to state, what follows may not be applicable in your state. Consult your state attorney general or federal wage and hour offices or employment offices for information specific to your area.

- **The Civil Rights Act of 1964/Title Seven Amendment of 1967:** These federal laws and their subsequent amendments prohibit employment discrimination on the basis of race; color; religion; sex (includes pregnancy and related medical conditions and marital status of a woman); marriage to a person of another racial, religious, or ethnic group; national origin or ancestry; physical or mental disability; medical condition; or veteran status. Currently, employers with 15 or more employees are covered. Age discrimination is prohibited by the Age Discrimination in Employment Act of 1975. Some states prohibit employment discrimination on the basis of sexual orientation.
- **The Equal Pay Act of 1963:** This federal law prohibits pay differences based only on sex. That is, paying employees "at a rate less than the rate at which the employer pays wages to employees of the opposite sex in such establishments for equal work on jobs the performance of which require equal skill, effort, and responsibility and which are performed under similar working conditions" is unlawful. The statute has been interpreted to prohibit pay discrimination on the basis of race, religion, or national origin as well.
- **Immigration Reform and Control Act of 1986:** This act makes it unlawful for private employers with three or more employees to discriminate on the basis of national origin and citizenship, unless the person is an illegal alien. The act also required that every employee complete an Employment Eligibility Verification form, commonly referred to as an I-9 form, which certifies that employee is eligible to

work in the United States and has produced documents to prove that eligibility. (A sample Employment Eligibility Verification form is reproduced on pages 74–75)

- **Employment of Minors:** In most states, employees under 18 years of age must present a work permit signed by the juvenile court judge who has jurisdiction for the county or city where the minor lives or is applying for work and/or by the principal or counselor of the school the employee attends.
- **Church School Staff Employment:** The federal government has given the states jurisdiction over church preschool programs, usually the department of social services or division of licensing. Since each state has different laws and guidelines governing preschool programs, I suggest that you contact your state's department of social services for the laws and guidelines you are required to follow for your church's program. Church schools for grades one and up are usually overseen by a state department of education.

Hiring Church Members

If you employ someone who is already a member of your congregation, the pastor and church officers should ensure that she or he receive the same compensation, working conditions, and so forth as a nonmember. In my experience with churches, members generally make good employees (much as relatives of good employees do in secular organizations). However, recognize that there is an inherent danger in employing a member of your church if it ever became necessary to terminate the employment of that individual. Regardless of how professionally you handle the termination, other family and church members will be affected. Following the process explained in this chapter will improve your likelihood of making sound staff employment decisions and avoiding problems, whether the employee is a member or not.

Screening Job Applicants

One person on the search committee, preferably someone with a background in human resources, should be assigned the responsibility for screening resumes and employment applications, especially for professional positions. Note that applicants for housekeeper (janitorial) openings will often not have a resume, so it will be necessary to mail an employment application to these applicants (see the sample Employment Application form on page 69).

The person responsible for screening resumes and employment applications should also be responsible for phoning applicants when there is a need to clarify information arising from the review of those forms. Prior to the search committee meeting to finalize selection of applicants to be interviewed, members should be given copies of the resumes or employment applications of those who will be considered further.

Employment Interviewing

I have found that the following process works well when interviewing job candidates, while presenting some attractive options according to the hiring situation:

- **Step 1—Determining Questions:** Prior to beginning interviews, the search committee chair should determine the questions that will be asked of applicants by each committee member.
- **Step 2—Introductions:** Since committee interviews can be awkward for the interviewee, I suggest that the chair start the interviews by introducing herself or himself and the committee members. To further relax the applicant, restate the job duties and other employment particulars.
- **Step 3—Interview Techniques:** The objective of the interview process is to select the applicant who is qualified for the position (someone who has the necessary job skills and education to perform the described duties), has the ability to work well with the staff, is dependable and conscientiousness, and has good work history stability. I suggest two interview techniques:

  Directed—Ask the applicant direct questions concerning her or his resume and employment application, as well as questions arising out of the screening process.
  Nondirected—After the applicant is asked a question, she or he answers without further intervention from the committee member asking the question. This technique enables the interviewer to probe the ability of the applicant to organize her or his thoughts. Questions could include:

  Why did you apply for this position?
  What employment experiences have you had that would help you be successful in this position?

26

This technique would be especially helpful when interviewing professional or salaried applicants whose jobs may require greater verbal skills.

- **Step 4—Close:** To close the interview, tell the applicant when she or he can expect to receive feedback regarding the selection decision and that you will conduct an employment background check as well as a retail credit and criminal investigation if they are finalists. This is also a good time to obtain or verify employer contact information for references and to obtain their consent for contacting former employers (see the Employment Reference Inquiry form on page 72). Present each applicant with your employee handbook, which is a good way to reinforce information given to the applicant during the interview (see the sample Employee Handbook beginning on page 101).

  Each search committee member should prepare a summary report noting her or his impression of an interviewee immediately following each interview. If the committee has interviewed more than one applicant, the search committee should openly discuss each candidate. The committee chair can then collect report forms from each member to help identify which applicants are the most qualified for further employment consideration. Applicants who are finalists for a position should have their employment backgrounds investigated by either the personnel liaison or a search committee member.

- **Step 5—Background Investigation:** The most meaningful employment contacts are phone calls to the immediate supervisors of an applicant. However, the applicant's present employer should be contacted for an employment reference only after the applicant accepts your verbal employment offer, especially if she or he has been with that employer for two or more years. Applicants should obviously be told that you are going to contact their present employer regarding employment information. If you phone the human resource department of an applicant's former employer, you will normally learn only that person's position at separation and the dates of her or his employment for fear of legal reprisals for disqualifying information.

  Use the employment reference investigation form (see page 71) when investigating employment information. The most pertinent employment background information is normally the five years of employment history preceding the date of application for your job opening.

- **Step 6—Final Employee Selection:** After employment references are completed and deemed satisfactory, the applicant selected for employment should be phoned with a verbal employment offer, followed by a typed offer letter, federal and state W4 forms, an I-9 form (see page 74), and applicable insurance forms. These all should be returned with a copy of the offer letter signed by the new employee.

Applicants not selected should also be notified. Do not attempt to explain to an applicant why she or he was not offered the position or rejected. Simply thank the applicant for applying; there is no need to go any further.

- **Step 7—Communication to Bookkeeper and Staff Personnel Coordinator:** The personnel action notice form (see page 76) should be completed by the search committee chair and given to the bookkeeper or personnel coordinator in order to enter the new employee into the church payroll and records system. Your secretary or staff personnel coordinator should establish a personnel file folder for each employee where all employment and personnel-related forms are retained. You are required by federal law to keep employment applications for one year from your church's date of receipt. It is a good practice to have your secretary purge this file annually.

- **Step 8—Communication with the Congregation:** The final step of the employment process should be to have the search committee chair announce the person selected to fill the opening to the congregation at the worship service following your employment decision and in your next newsletter.

Employee Orientation and Training

The best time to orient a new employee is on her or his first day on the job (see the Employee Orientation Procedure and the Employee Orientation Checklist on page 77). The new employee's immediate supervisor should conduct the orientation. Make use of the employee handbook, the position's job description, applicable insurance booklets, and any other relevant information about the church for this process. Since it is desirable to combine the employee orientation process with the initial training of a new employee, I recommend this brief training strategy:

1. The supervisor of the new employee should have primary responsibility for her or his orientation and training.
2. A current job description for the position can be used for training the new employee.

3. If the departing employee is leaving on favorable terms and would be an effective trainer, it is desirable to have her or him spend two or three days training the new employee.
4. Consider training the new employee by utilizing this four-step training method:
   a. *Explain* (using a current job description, the trainer explains job duties);
   b. *Demonstrate* (trainee repeats her or his understanding of job tasks);
   c. *Try out* (have employee perform job tasks);and
   d. *Correct* (trainer corrects any tasks not performed correctly). Also, explain how this job relates to overall support of your church and its office function.

If you follow the principles outlined in this chapter, your church should not only employ a productive and stable staff but also be known in your community as being a good place to work.

CHAPTER 4

Church Staff Goals: What's Possible and Reasonable?

Three years after first becoming pastor at Stone Church, Bruce had his first performance evaluation. The Focus and Direction Task Force (F & D) spent more than three hours preparing the evaluation because there were no measurable goals in place by which his job performance could be judged. Only one year earlier, Bruce had developed a job description for himself, but without any input from the church officers

The church staff found themselves in a similar situation. They had not developed any job goals, so there were no standards by which to measure their work. Nor did they have up-to-date job descriptions that accurately reflected their actual work.

Seeing a problem, Ned developed a strategy to change the situation. He first suggested that each church committee develop detailed, measurable church goals for the coming fiscal year, after which F & D would convene to discuss these documents. When F & D met, they consolidated the goals submitted by each committee into a single goals document, from which they in turn developed church-wide goals. In addition, they formulated a mission statement for the church based on Bruce's and the officers' vision of how the congregation could grow in quality and quantity so as to better serve Christ.

Bruce then developed a draft of his personal job goals based on the consolidated church-wide goals document from F & D. Under Bruce's direction, the choir, Christian education, and preschool directors, along with the church bookkeeper and secretary, each developed their own performance goals, as well as personal development goals, all based on the other goals documents. By an assigned date, all the staff members returned their goals document to Bruce for review.

After receiving these documents, Bruce met with each person individually to discuss, amend through negotiation, and finalize their respective goals drafts. He then incorporated into his own goals those staff goals requiring action on his part to enable staff members to accomplish their goals.

Having completed these tasks, Bruce met with F & D to negotiate his own goals. They made minor changes to his document, which he modified on the basis of their recommendations. The secretary then typed the final versions of his goals and those of the other staff members affected on the goals performance evaluation form. Bruce then met individually with each staff member and gave each a copy of the job performance goals document (see page 91). He also explained how future salary increases would be based on goals accomplishment, since Stone Church officers had chosen to adopt the merit salary award system (see chapter 5).

As a result of this strategy, F & D members now have a system in place that will enable them to monitor more easily the job performances of Bruce and the other staff who participate in the goals process during the church fiscal year. They can also more objectively evaluate and reward the accomplishment of individual goals at the end of the year.

A Pastor's Perspective on Church Mission Statements

The writer of Proverbs tells us, "Where there is no vision the people perish" (Proverbs 29:18). So it is for the structure of the church: A clearly articulated vision is the first step to everything.

Most progressive businesses today have a mission statement that they put in their employee handbooks and display in conspicuous places for employees and the public. A mission statement focuses on an organization's vision, emphasis, and major goals or objectives. It is part of a strategy to achieve a positive business-employee climate and to maximize profitability (or cost containment for not-for-profit businesses).

Mission Statement Development

If your church currently does not have a mission statement, the following process will help you develop one:

- **Step 1:** The officers and each committee of the church's governing body should develop goals for a calendar or fiscal year.
- **Step 2:** F & D or church officers develop a composite of the committee goals into a single document written in language that can be easily understood by the church officers, congregation, and staff. I suggest

that the goals on the final document be listed in the order in which the officers feel they contribute to the church's mission (most impact to least impact).

- **Step 3:** F & D or church officers develop a mission statement based on that consolidated document. As noted in chapter 1, your statement should also include goals of your denomination and the ultimate goal of serving Christ.
- **Step 4:** Once finalized, the mission statement is communicated to the church's membership, displayed for visitors and members to see in the church vestibule, and included in all church publications.

Staff Goals

At the point in my career that I became a senior corporate officer and was able to effect policy, I gained respect for Management by Objectives (MBO) as an integral component in managing a business. MBO developed as a business management strategy in the 1950s and has been used in one form or another by most results-driven and profitable organizations.

MBO systems have had a significant impact on employee motivation and morale, operating effectiveness, and ultimately the profitability and/or cost containment of every organization with which I have been associated. In tune with current usage, I have elected in this book to use the term *goals,* which is synonymous with objectives.

I can assure you that your church staff will become more results oriented after one year with a goals system in place. The goals system works in tandem with the salary administration and performance evaluation systems, which are explained later in this chapter and in chapter 5.

Developing Staff Goals

I recommend that you follow these steps when developing goals for your church staff.

- **Step 1:** Each staff member develops her or his own job description (see chapter 2 and the sample job description on page 67). Job descriptions must be written before goals can be developed by participating staff members. I recommend this for all salaried or professional positions, including ordained staff, the music director, Christian education director, preschool director, secretary or administrative manager, and bookkeeper.

- **Step 2:** A goal is then written for each major task listed on the job descriptions.
- **Step 3:** F & D or church officers meet to approve and/or negotiate changes to the senior pastor's goals.
- **Step 4:** The senior pastor then meets individually with those staff persons participating in the goal-setting process and undertakes a review and negotiation of the goals they have submitted.
- **Step 5:** After F & D gives final approval to the pastor's and staff's goals, each staff person types her or his goals on the job performance goals form (see sample goals on page 91) and distributes copies of this document to her or his supervisor and to F & D or the church officers.
- **Step 6:** The administration committee and its budget development subcommittee meet to plan the church's annual budget based on staff goals, committee programs, and other activities planned for the new fiscal year.
- **Step 7:** I recommend that F & D or the church officers meet in the middle of the fiscal year to assess the church staff's accomplishment of its goals and to revise those documents as needed. Such factors as changes in revenues received during the first six months of the fiscal year, program additions or deletions, and so forth may necessitate such changes.

Performance Factors Evaluation System

I suggest that you adopt the Performance Evaluation and Improvement Plan form (see page 92) for your housekeeper or janitor, clerk or data entry specialist, organist, and other hourly paid staff. (Follow the suggested performance evaluation procedure explained in Policy 605.0, page 86.)

CHAPTER 5

The "Carrot & Stick": Staff Evaluation and Compensation Policies

One year later the Stone Church officers had approved a new personnel system, which included policies and procedures governing salary and performance evaluation, administration, and discipline. Having established a performance goals evaluation system, the Focus & Direction Task Force (F & D), with input from each of its governing committees, prepared Pastor Bruce's second annual performance evaluation in half the time as the first evaluation the previous year. F & D also gave Bruce a midyear evaluation; Bruce also administered midyear performance evaluations to his staff.

Because Bruce was evaluated by goals that he and F & D had developed together, there were no surprises when he was evaluated by this system. Since this was the third performance evaluation F & D had given to Bruce (counting the midyear evaluation) they felt they had a handle on administering this system. Therefore they added the "outstanding" rating category to his evaluation form for this evaluation and increased his salary by 7 percent.

Bruce presented to F & D drafts of the performance evaluations he had prepared for each staff member. Bruce had given an overall rating of "excellent" to each of his staff members except his secretary, whom he evaluated as "outstanding," and the new choir director, Barbara, who was given a "too early to rate"on her evaluation because she was, according to Bruce, still in a "personal growth mode."

The process of getting through these successful evaluations was not without difficulty, however. Earlier in the year, after several counseling sessions with the choir director, Marjorie, about her job performance problems, Pastor Bruce had come to grips with the fact that he had to deal with her problem in a more formal fashion. Because he considered other matters more worthy of his time, he had elected not to administer the midyear performance evaluations for the staff as outlined in the personnel policy.

Bruce met with the worship committee chair, Mary, to get her input and advice regarding the music program predicament. He then phoned Ned and the administration committee chair, Tim, to arrange a meeting to discuss staff wage increases, which were to be effective January 1.

Bruce began the meeting by explaining his attempts to help Marjorie correct her job deficiencies, which have resulted in the loss of several seasoned choir members. Mary had already recommended Marjorie's termination to Bruce.

Ned asked Bruce, "Did you give Marjorie her semiannual performance evaluation explaining her job deficiencies?" Bruce answered, "No." "Have you given her a written warning as explained in the discipline policy, using the performance evaluation form?" asked Ned. Again, Bruce replied, "No." Ned then explained to Bruce that in order to be fair to Marjorie and to protect the church from potential legal exposure since the discipline policy had not been followed, Bruce should prepare and administer a written warning to Marjorie at once.

Having learned that Bruce had not conducted midyear staff performance evaluations, Ned advised Bruce to prepare year-end performance evaluations for each staff member so the personnel committee could determine the salary awards the staff should receive. Ned further advised Bruce that no salary increase would be considered for Marjorie.

Two days later Bruce, Ned, and Mary met to review the performance evaluation warning Bruce prepared to present to Marjorie. They agreed that Bruce would inform Marjorie that she would be reviewed again in 30 days via the performance evaluation to assess her progress in improving her job deficiencies. She also would be told that she would not receive a salary increase at the time of her warning and evaluation.

Thirty days later, after Bruce had given Marjorie a warning as part of her performance evaluation for her work over the past year, her overall evaluation is still "unsatisfactory." After considerable mental anguish, reflection, and discussion, Bruce, Ned, Mary, and Tim agreed that it was unlikely that Marjorie would improve her performance, even if given a second "unsatisfactory" performance evaluation and warning. They decided to terminate Marjorie.

Bruce and Ned met with Marjorie in her office to inform her of their decision (they decided to meet in Marjorie's office so they could leave after taking action and minimize the awkwardness of the situation). Bruce, as Marjorie's supervisor, asked Ned, an experienced human resource director, to lead the termination session since he had never terminated an employee. Such a strategy also enables Bruce to maintain an "arm's length" position in the termination procedure. At the meeting, after a brief statement Ned presented Marjorie with the severance arrangement, including pay, benefits, and an employment reference statement she could give to prospective employers. He also offered Marjorie out-placement assistance, if she desired.

A Pastor's Perspective on Theology and Ethics

In Matthew 18:15-20, Jesus tells us how to deal with conflict in the life of the church. While there are certainly times to deal with issues and concerns on a one-on-one basis, there are also times when we need to involve others. Nowhere is this more important than in our dealings with issues among the staff. All too often one-on-one contact, especially when it deals with concerns and correction, can blow up in the face of the church. Miscommunication and misunderstanding all too often result. Just as Jesus encourages us to involve others when there is a conflict, so should our approach to personnel management have a clearly outlined approach to dealing with conflict. Such a set of policies seeks to maintain confidentially yet involves enough people so that no one person is saddled with too much personal responsibility.

Employee Performance Evaluations

I have learned from experience that once goals are in place, especially for salaried staff, you have the basis for evaluating job performance achievement more objectively and fairly. (As mentioned in chapter 4, the Performance Evaluation and Improvement Plan for Nonordained Staff on page 92 is recommended for your nonsalaried staff, such as housekeeper/janitor, data entry clerk, and organist/pianist.) The performance evaluation process is one of the most powerful tools you can use in promoting employee job performance excellence and commitment. It is also key to building positive morale among your church staff and creating harmony between your staff, officers, and congregation.

The appendix provides you with three performance evaluation forms: two separate Performance Evaluation and Improvement Plan forms for nonordained (page 92) and ordained (page 93) staff and a Job Performance Goals form for ordained staff and professional nonordained staff (page 95). I have found that the optimum interval for evaluating employee job performance, regardless of position, is *every six months* (at the middle and end of the fiscal year or in June and December of the calendar year).

If you do not now have a performance evaluation system in place or if you are beyond the beginning of your fiscal year when you implement your performance evaluation system, I recommend that you adopt the performance factors system to get started, since it does not require you to develop goals with someone you supervise (as explained later in this chapter). Keep in mind, however, that using a goals system is the most effective strategy for enhancing employee performance excellence. Therefore, I recommend that you adopt the Job Performance Goals evaluation form when you can begin the process at the beginning of a new fiscal year or when your human resource professional or personnel liaison feels you are ready to do so.

Conducting Effective Performance Evaluations

*   **Step 1:** Give the persons you supervise the performance factors or performance goals by which she or he will be evaluated at the time you adopt the performance evaluation process. It is also good practice to discuss these factors or goals during the orientation of a new employee.
*   **Step 2:** Tell the staff member when the evaluation will take place so that she or he can prepare for it. Select a place for the evaluation that is private, with no interruptions, but that is also informal (if practical, do not sit across a desk from your subordinate). The climate for your feedback session is as important as the evaluation itself.
*   **Step 3:** Evaluate each factor or goal and then write out a narrative statement summarizing that evaluation. The performance evaluation form is designed so that the evaluation can be done on page one and the narrative statement summarizing that evaluation can be written on page two. I recommend that you use the categories of "Excellent," "Good," "Marginal," "Unsatisfactory," or "Too Early to Rate" for each factor or goal the first time you implement a performance evaluation system. The "Outstanding" rating category should not be added to the evaluation form until after the performance evaluation process has been in place for one to two years in order for the pastor and other supervisors not experienced with administering performance evaluations to gain experience with the process.
*   **Step 4:** Review how you rated each performance factor or goal and the contents of each performance narrative before you determine the over-

all rating. Don't assign an overall rating based solely on the total number of marks (x) in a rating category, since certain factors should carry greater weight than others. For example, your rating for "quality of work" should be given greater weight than that for "personal appearance." It is important to remember that any performance evaluation has a degree of subjectivity; the process explained here is designed to enhance the evaluator's objectivity.

- **Step 5:** An alternative strategy you can employ at a midyear evaluation is to have the subordinate prepare a self-evaluation prior to your conference. The pastor or supervisor would also prepare an evaluation of the subordinate before meeting with the employee. When utilizing this self-evaluation strategy, allow the subordinate to present her or his evaluation *first*. After the subordinate finishes, you (the supervisor) would then present your evaluation.

- **Step 6:** Since there is always a great deal of anxiety at the time of a subordinate's evaluation, especially the first, obtain the subordinate's undivided attention by informing her or him of the overall rating at the beginning of the evaluation, *if* the rating is "Good," "Excellent," or (eventually) "Outstanding." *If,* however, the overall rating is "Marginal" or "Unsatisfactory," it is more effective to evaluate each factor or goal as you progress through the evaluation form. Such a strategy will enable you to coach the subordinate as to how she or he can improve each "Marginal" and/or "Unsatisfactory" performance factor or goal. Obviously, you want to offer praise to your subordinate for "Excellent," "Good," and "Outstanding" ratings.

  It is critical that you be candid and accurate when administering a performance evaluation with a subordinate. As a means of ensuring accuracy when conveying facts or information about job performance, it is good practice to maintain a file folder for each subordinate. When you observe a subordinate's action or inaction that affects her or his job performance either positively or negatively, write a brief note, date it, and drop it into their file. Later, when you begin preparing performance evaluations, you will have accurate information on hand to draw upon.

- **Step 7:** Remember, if you are to improve the job performance of a subordinate, the evaluation must be a two-way dialogue. Avoid being defensive; permit a subordinate to disagree with your evaluation of a performance factor or goal; be flexible. Changing one or two ratings of a factor or goal should not change the overall rating, however. Again, the objective of the evaluation process is to improve the subordinate's job performance. The result is a "win-win" situation!

Employee Counseling and Warnings

The performance evaluation document can be used at times other than semi-annual reviews to provide you with an instrument with which to address problems or recognize achievements. This can be an ideal, informal way to improve morale or to deal with difficulties before they become destructive situations. As explained in chapter 3, federal laws may favor an employee in matters of termination, especially if employer discrimination can be proven by the EEOC or Labor Department when representing a terminated employee. It is therefore necessary for you as an employer to protect your church against a disgruntled terminated employee who could seek legal recourse.

Administering a written warning to an employee for poor job performance or for an infraction of a church policy will lessen the possibility of your church being formally charged by a federal or state agency for an unjust employee termination (see Employee Discipline, Policy 603.0, on page 79). Since the same performance evaluation form (whether "performance factors" or "performance goals") is used for administering both employee warnings and semiannual performance evaluations, I must add two additional points to the above instructions on conducting effective performance evaluations.

First, when administrating a written warning, the overall rating must be either "Marginal" or "Unsatisfactory" in order to convey the seriousness of your warning to the subordinate. Obviously, an overall rating of "Unsatisfactory" conveys a stronger message than "Marginal." Second, you should never award a salary increase at the same time that you give an employee a warning under any circumstance, since doing so conveys to the employee that her or his performance is really satisfactory (see Employee Discipline, Policy 603.0 on page 79, regarding the administration of an employee warning).

I recommend that you state both on the "next evaluation date" blank (page one of the Performance Evaluation and Improvement Plan form) and in the "performance narrative" section (page two of the form) the time period (one to three months as determined by the circumstance) that the subordinate is given to improve her or his performance before the next evaluation is to be administered. Place that date on your calendar so you do not overlook the follow-up evaluation.

Employee Exit Interview Process

The purpose of the exit interview policy is not only to prevent the turnover of other employees by finding out why the employee resigned, it can also be used to convince an employee who is leaving your church voluntarily not to leave after all. It does not serve a useful purpose to "exit interview" an employee who has been terminated for cause (see Employee Exit Interview, Policy 606.0, on page 97). Distribute exit interview report copies to the pastor, church officers, or F & D members and place a copy in the file of the employee.

Out-Placement Process

The purpose of the out-placement process is to help an employee who, in most cases, has been terminated involuntarily find other employment and to convey a sense of concern for the employee even in such an awkward situation. Only attempt out-placement assistance for a terminated employee if a human resource professional serves as your personnel liaison or personnel committee chair and is willing to function as the facilitator for such counseling.

Salary and Benefit Plan Administration

Another important component of your church's personnel program is the administration of staff salaries and benefits for both nonordained and ordained personnel. As you realize, the salary an individual is paid has the psychological means of motivating or not motivating that person, so it is important to pay employees competitively, equitably with other church jobs, and commensurate with responsibility and job performance.

The recommended format for your church's salary ranges is to have a minimum, maximum, and a midpoint (the salary midway between the minimum and maximum salary as determined by salary-benefit survey data). The midpoint is the salary an experienced (three to five years) employee should be paid. (For a further explanation of salary ranges and their use in administering salaries/wages, see Salary and Performance Evaluation Administration, Policy 605.0, on page 86). Note that I have used "salary" instead of "wage" to minimize confusion; when conducting a salary and benefit survey you may find that "salary" applies to ordained and/or professional positions while "wage" is used for nonordained and/or clerical positions.

If your church does not have the expertise to determine salary ranges, a consultant such as the author can help you develop this essential personnel tool.

Conducting a Salary and Benefit Survey

Your personnel liaison or a member of the personnel committee (preferably an individual with human resource experience) should conduct a salary and benefit survey annually. This is commonly referred to by human resource professionals as a "market compensation survey," and is based on the salaries paid and benefits provided for jobs in your given market (denomination, geographic area, job classification, and so forth). Note that there are other methods for developing salary ranges, such as job evaluation, which is a method of determining salary values based on comparative responsibilities for jobs, as well as other criteria. I have chosen to use the "market" method here because I feel it is the most practical and accurate and the easiest to use in developing salary ranges.

In order to determine the compensation (salary and benefits) package your church should provide to be competitive and fair, make a list of the contacts to survey. In most churches the secretary is the best person to contact to obtain salary and benefit information. In large churches the secretary may refer you to the chair of the personnel committee. Churches of your own denomination will gladly give or exchange salary and benefit information with you; contact your denomination's regional offices as well. When contacting churches of other denominations, if you detect hesitation in giving you salary and benefit data, offer to exchange your salary and benefit data for theirs. Your state employment services and the local Chamber of Commerce will willingly provide you with their salary survey data, but always ask when the survey was taken; if salary or benefit data is over two years old, it may not be relevant.

The *Compensation Handbook for Church Staff* is an annual, comprehensive, ecumenical survey of ordained and nonordained staff salary and benefit data published by Christian Ministry Resources (CMR). This excellent resource breaks out its information for full-time positions by: "Worship Attendance," "Budget," "Church Setting (Community)-Worship Attendance," "Education," and "Years Employed"; part-time positions are broken-out by hours worked per week. CMR's *Handbook* also offers other useful data such as the national salary average by position for each of the preceding five years. (To obtain this book, contact Christian Ministry Resources, P.O. Box 1098, Matthews, NC, 28106; telephone (704) 841-8039.)

Merit vs. Flat Salary Increase Systems

A merit pay system is designed to reward a larger pay increase to an employee who earns an overall performance rating of, for example, "Excellent" than she or he would for an overall performance rating of "Good." A merit salary system could be better suited for churches that are *not* having difficulty increasing their annual budgeted income/pledges (for an example, see step 5 in the staff salary administration process below.).

A flat salary award system, if adopted, would grant the *same* salary increase to *all* employees, ordained and nonordained, who achieve at least a "Good" overall evaluation. These increases could be tied to the national cost of living index; for example, 3 percent salary increases would be granted for a year when the cost of living increased by 3 percent.

Staff Salary Administration Process

- **Step 1:** Distribute a copy of the salary range document to the pastor, personnel liaison, or personnel committee chair, and the secretary or the staff person who serves as the personnel coordinator.
- **Step 2:** The personnel liaison or personnel committee chair educates the secretary/personnel coordinator concerning her or his role in administering performance evaluations and salary awards. (The secretary distributes the appropriate performance evaluation form to the supervisor of the employee to be evaluated one month prior to the date on which the evaluation is to take place.)
- **Step 3:** When a salary award is determined for an employee and approved by the appropriate church officers, the personnel coordinator completes a Personnel Action Notice form and forwards a copy of same to the bookkeeper to initiate the salary increase.
- **Step 4:** The personnel liaison or personnel committee chair should update the salary ranges annually.
- **Step 5:** The personnel liaison would then determine the salary awards percentage that would be available for each of the overall performance rating categories that are eligible for increases ("Outstanding," "Excellent," and "Good"). A 2 to 3 percent differential between overall performance rating categories is sufficient to motivate employees to

enhance job performance or goals obtainment. For example, employees would receive the salary awards listed below if a merit salary system were adopted:

OVERALL RATING	INCREASE	APPLICATION
Outstanding	7%	Superlative performers; one or two staff members only
Excellent	5%	Performance consistently *exceeds* goals or job performance factors
Good	3%	Cost-of-living adjustment

For more information, see Salary & Performance Evaluation Administration, Policy 605.0, on page 86.

CHAPTER 6

Achieving Staff and Officer Harmony: Assessing Committee, Officer, and Staff Morale

Jean has been secretary at Stone Church for 12 years, a member of the church for 11 years, and is regarded by Bruce, the staff, and the congregation as an exemplary employee. Bruce arrived early Monday morning and began opening his mail. Much to his surprise he found a letter from Jean announcing her resignation from the staff and from the church. Stone Church had experienced some staff changes during Bruce's three-year tenure, but employee turnover has been attributed to poor employee selection and not having a personnel system. Jean's leaving the staff would certainly "raise the eyebrows" of the membership.

Bruce called Ned at work and informed him of Jean's resignation. In addition to the problems leading to the termination of Marjorie, the choir director, Chuck, Jean's husband, had also decided in the past year that it was time for him to resign as Christian Education Director (CED). As a result, Bruce had been inundated with having to do both his and Chuck's jobs. In spite of his positive job reviews, the church officers felt that Bruce had somehow contributed to these staff turnovers.

To lighten his load, Bruce had assigned some of the Chuck's administrative work to Jean three months ago. At the time that Chuck left the staff Ned recommended that a temporary data entry clerk be employed until a new CED could be hired. Bruce did not feel it was necessary to recruit a temporary employee to assist Jean, commenting to Ned, "Jean can handle the additional work." Ned told Bruce he had sensed something was bothering Jean for the past couple of months but did not take time to speak with her privately about his perception.

Bruce met with Jean the day he received her resignation. Bruce asked Jean to reconsider her decision to resign, and she agreed to think about it. Bruce told Ned he did not feel she would change her mind. Ned then decided to meet with Jean the next day, not only to conduct her exit interview, as required by policy, but also to attempt to retain her as an employee and church member. Ned discovered during this conference that Jean's concerns had been building for some time; the additional assignment of Chuck's administrative work with no replacement or relief in sight was the last straw prompting her resignation. Jean also informed Ned about other concerns, including poor office work station arrangements that caused work inefficiency and staff communication problems. Jean had not informed Bruce of these concerns because she felt he would be insensitive to correcting the situations.

After meeting with Jean, Ned met with Bruce and they decided to announce together to Jean that they wanted her to contact a temporary employment service that day for a part-time data entry clerk. Fortunately, because of the immediate attention to Jean's concern by Bruce and Ned, Jean withdrew her resignations. Shortly thereafter, Ned spoke with Bruce and the Focus and Direction Task Force (F & D) about conducting a staff opinion survey in order to assess their attitudes toward Bruce and church personnel policies. Ned's request was approved.

After conducting a one-on-one, confidential staff opinion survey, Ned analyzed the results, which revealed that staff members had a relationship problem with Bruce, as well as concerns about church personnel policies and practices, including workload issues. Ned presented a summary of the staff survey first to Bruce and then to F & D, along with recommendations for addressing the identified issues. F & D approved the recommended actions offered by Bruce and Ned.

A Pastor's Perspective on Theology and Ethics

> Paul speaks to the Corinthian Christians about the different gifts that we bring to the church (1 Corinthians 12-14). A large mistake many churches make is to assume that the pastor will have the gift of personnel management. Unfortunately, seminaries don't give much help in teaching our pastors how to develop effective staff relationships, and often the gifts of pastors are not best suited to dealing with staff conflict. Every congregation, however, regardless of its size, will have within it people who do have such gifts. Use them!

Employee Morale Assessment

It is wise to have the personnel liaison or a personnel committee member survey the staff at least every two years (or annually, if you are experiencing high employee turnover or unrest). Before you make this decision to conduct a survey with your staff, it is essential that you consider the following:

1. An opinion survey must never be undertaken if the pastor and church officers are not willing to face and correct problems that may be voiced by the staff. Such inaction will only make matters worse!
2. The person selected to conduct the survey (preferably the personnel liaison or an officer possessing professional human resource experience) should not be the pastor or another staff member. Only a person considered "neutral" and who is trusted by the staff should conduct the survey.
3. In order to obtain candid responses, the survey participants must be assured by the interviewer that their responses will be kept anonymous and confidential.
4. Survey questions should be written out to ensure that the interviewer asks the same questions of each participant. They should be written in a positive manner so that negative responses are only made when the employee's relationship with the pastor or supervisor or her or his opinions of the church's personnel policies and practices are not favorable (for instance, "Do you have a positive relationship with the pastor?" not "Do you have problems in your relationship with the pastor?").
5. After the survey results are analyzed, the personnel liaison or personnel committee chair should meet with the pastor to review the survey summary and decide what actions are needed, if any, to improve the pastor's relationship with the staff or to modify personnel policies or practices that are viewed unfavorably.
6. The pastor and personnel liaison should meet with the staff within one month from the date of the survey to explain what actions will be taken to improve relationships, personnel policies, and/or practices they have reported as requiring improvement.

Churches with large staffs and without the expertise to conduct an opinion survey may want to contact a consultant such as the author for assistance.

Office Efficiency

If your church has not assessed its office layout and the equipment it uses recently, it may be time—or past time—to do so. The layout of the office work space and the equipment used in it not only affects employee efficiency, it can have a negative impact on employee morale and health as well.

Committee and Officer Effectiveness Surveys

Each year, the administration committee chair (or an officer selected by the pastor) should distribute a survey to all church committee members to determine the effectiveness of the committees, their chairs, and the ordained staff (see the Annual Committee Survey of Service Experience on page 100). The officer responsible for this survey should prepare a report on each committee as well a summary report on all committees. Church officers should also be surveyed annually to assess their relationships with the ordained and nonordained staff (see the Annual Officer Survey of Service Experience on page 99). The officer responsible for this survey should also prepare a summary report, which should be given to every officer/F & D member, as well as the pastor.

CHAPTER 7

Managing the Personnel System

Ned has integrated Stone Church's new personnel policies, procedures, and forms with its existing policies and distributed a copy of the revised personnel manual to the Focus and Direction Task Force (F & D), the preschool director, and to Pastor Bruce. Once they had reviewed these, Ned conducted a briefing with the lay officers and pastor regarding these new personnel policies and procedures and forms in order to educate those who would be involved with personnel administration matters.

Ned held a more in-depth briefing with Jean, the secretary, because of her role as personnel coordinator. Jean was then given the responsibility to brief Brenda, the part-time bookkeeper, regarding her involvement with the new personnel system.

Two years after beginning this adoption of a new personnel system, reviewing the year-end statistics received from the administration committee was a cause for elation for F & D: Worship service attendance was up 8 percent over the previous year versus a goal of 7 percent; membership was up 5 percent versus a goal of 7 percent; pledge giving was up 6 percent versus a goal of 5 percent; Sunday School attendance was up 4 percent versus a goal of 5 percent; preschool enrollment was up 7 percent versus a goal of 8 percent; choir membership was up 3 percent versus a goal of 5 percent. Moreover, Stone Church had experienced no staff turnover in over a year and the work done on the majority of the other goals was evaluated as either "Excellent" or "Outstanding." Other churches took notice and consulted with Stone Church about their personnel practices. It was a difficult road, but Stone Church knew it was well on the way to being a better place to work and a thriving community of faith.

Personnel System Administration

Responsibilities for initiating and administering actions or activities related to the personnel system are identified below, as well as those duties and goals noted in the job descriptions of ordained and nonordained staff:

SYSTEM COMPONENT	INITIATING RESPONSIBILITY	FINAL RESPONSIBILITY
Job Design and Specifications	Personnel Liaison	Sr. Pastor
Job Descriptions	Each employee	Sr. Pastor
Goals	Selected employees	F & D/Officers and Sr. Pastor

Policies and Procedures:

Personnel Philosophy	Personnel Liaison	F & D/Officers and Sr. Pastor
Policy Development	Administration Chair	Sr. Pastor and/or Personnel Liaison
Job Classifications	Personnel Liaison	Sr. Pastor
Employee Benefit Plan	Personnel Liaison	F & D/Officers
Employee Fair Treatment	Personnel Liaison	Sr. Pastor

Employment:

Application Form	Personnel Liaison	Chair, Search Committees
Reference Investigation	Personnel Liaison	Chair, Search Committees
Offer Confirmation Letter	Personnel Liaison	Chair, Search Committees
Employee Discipline	Sr. Pastor /Supervisor	F & D/Officers and Personnel Liaison
Employee Leave of Absence	Sr. Pastor	F & D/Officers
Employee Perf. Evaluation	Secretary/Adm. Mgr.	Sr. Pastor; F & D/Officers
Employee Salary Adm.	Secretary/Adm. Mgr.	Sr. Pastor; F & D/Officers
Ordained Staff Work Week	Personnel Liaison	F & D/Officers
Employee Exit Interview/Outplacement	Personnel Liaison	F & D/Officers

Personnel Action Notice

The Personnel Action Notice (PAN) is the instrument designed to assist the secretary or personnel coordinator in recording all personnel actions (for instance, hire date and job classification; salary increases; leaves of absence; marital status or name change; termination date and reason, and so forth) (see the sample on page 76) and communicating salary changes and leaves of absence to the bookkeeper. The individual initiating a personnel action should prepare a PAN for all such actions and provide copies to the pastor or immediate supervisor, the personnel liaison or personnel committee chair, and the employee's file. In the communication of salary and leave of absences actions, the bookkeeper should also receive a copy of the PAN.

Employee Record Keeping

- **Employee Active Files:** Now that you have the PAN to record all personnel actions, the personnel liaison or personnel committee chair should conduct an annual audit of your employee files to insure that you have an up-to-date file in place for each employee. I recommend that your secretary also serve as the personnel coordinator and maintain the employee files in her or his office area for accessibility. Keep them in a locked file cabinet for security and confidentiality.
- **Applicant Recruitment File:** As mentioned in chapter 3, you are required by federal law to retain employment applications of unsuccessful applicants for one year from date of application. It is good practice to purge this file every year.
- **Inactive Employee File:** I recommend that when someone leaves your employ, the secretary place the employee's complete file into an "inactive employee file" for future reference. There is no statutory time requirement for the retention of these files but it is recommended they be kept indefinitely.

Communications with Staff

To optimize communications between pastor and staff, I have found that scheduled individual conferences and weekly meetings with the entire staff are paramount.

Individual Conferences

I recommend that you meet with each subordinate every other week for one and one-half hours on the same day of the week. Depending on the size of your staff, such a process enables you to meet your staff within a half or whole day biweekly and helps maintain a sense of continuity. You should have a file folder for each subordinate (the same file for collecting performance evaluation information referred to in chapter 5). You can drop notes into an employee's file of topics you want to discuss at your next conference, which will help you prepare for these individual sessions.

To help your subordinates prepare for this biweekly conference with you, have them write out a list of the topics they want to discuss and/or seek counsel on in priority order. Request that they give you a copy of this agenda at the outset of each conference. If you have adopted the goals performance evaluation process for your subordinates, I suggest that you, as supervisor, review each employee's goals at least monthly to insure that she or he is on track.

Weekly Meetings

Schedule a weekly meeting with your entire staff on a regular day. Tuesdays often work well since Monday is usually a "catch up" day or, for many pastors, a day off. Begin the staff meetings first thing in the morning with no interruptions; find someone to volunteer as a receptionist to take messages during these meetings. Remember that the purpose of your weekly staff meeting is (1) to inform subordinates of upcoming events and activities for the week to ensure that each staff member is aware of her or his responsibilities; (2) to do problem solving for ongoing programs and activities; and (3) to seek input continually on improving the church administrative processes.

Annual Officer Strategic Plan Retreat

I recommend that you plan two officer retreats per year. The first, in the fall, is to develop your church's annual strategic plan and budget. In addition to all church officers, invite your ordained staff, the directors of the choir, Christian education, and preschool, and the secretary or administrative manager. As previously mentioned, the more you involve your secretary in church affairs, the better able she or he will be to assist you and anticipate your needs in accomplishing church goals.

A second retreat in the spring can serve to orient new officers and continue the development process for the other officers. Selected staff might also attend this retreat. The personnel liaison or personnel committee chair and the secretary should each be allotted time on the retreat agenda to brief officers regarding pertinent personnel policies and procedures.

In addition, scheduling a family retreat at least every other year, with an emphasis on Christian faith enrichment, is an effective means of enhancing commitment among your officers. Encourage all of your officers to attend along with their spouses. Don't forget to create special activities for the children and to have time for the families to play and worship together.

If you do not schedule a family retreat, consider hosting an informal cookout or picnic at your home for the officers, their spouses, and families. In the business world this is characterized as "team building." It is designed to enhance unity, commitment, and enthusiasm among those church members who will help you achieve the goals of your church and better serve our Lord.

Conclusion

You now have an understanding of how to construct a proven personnel system that, in just one or two years, will result in not only more stable, results-oriented staff members and officers but also improved relationships among the pastor, staff, officers, and congregation. Periodically reread this handbook to reinforce your understanding of these principles of effective personnel management and to enhance the climate of trust in your congregation. Ultimately, not only your community but also your worship and Sunday School visitors will sense that your church is different from others: a caring, loving, Christ-centered community of faith that works together for the betterment of the community and all the world.

Personnel Policies, Procedures, Practices, and Forms

The following appendixes contain policies and procedures, forms, and other information that will help you implement the personnel system described in this handbook in your own congregation. This material is laid out on the following pages, but it is also included on the CD-ROM that accompanies the handbook. The CD-ROM files are in two formats: (1) a Rich Text Format file (*.RTF) that you can open with many word processing programs, edit as you see appropriate, and print out for use with your personnel system; and (2) a Portable Document Format file (*.PDF) that you can print out using Adobe Acrobat, which is also included on the CD-ROM.

The following is a list of the appendixes, complete with page numbers on which they can be found and the names of the CD-ROM files where they can be accessed. The CD-ROM is used for storage purposes only. To access the file, simply select your CD-ROM drive and open as you would any file in the appropriate software. The file names correspond to the appendix numbers on the first page of each appendix.

A NOTE ON THE APPENDIXES

HOW TO INTEGRATE THE OLD PERSONNEL
SYSTEM INTO THE NEW

Not every policy, procedure, form, or strategy in this handbook can be adapted to your present personnel system. However, what is presented in this handbook represents a proven strategy from my own church personnel experiences.

In order to integrate your church's current personnel system with the system provided in this handbook with the least resistance from staff, officers, and congregation, the following strategy is recommended:

1. Assign one officer, preferably with human resource management experience who has demonstrated an ability to successfully implement new church programs, the task of installing your new personnel system.
2. Have the officer or the church secretary collect all known personnel policies and memoranda related to personnel administration and define in writing any *unwritten* personnel practices.
3. Everyone involved in the task of integrating your present personnel practices into the new personnel system should read this handbook in order to understand the rationale for the recommended actions.
4. Select a date for the pastor, the officer, and the secretary/administrative manager to meet to discuss the implementation process.
5. Have the personnel system facilitator review your new personnel system and proposed implementation plan with the church officers. This is best done with no other items of business on the meeting agenda to maximize consideration of the new personnel system.
6. When the Personnel Policy and Procedures Manual is completed, have the personnel system facilitator, with the pastor, review the highlights of the personnel system with the church staff. In addition, have the secretary/administrative manager issue copies to the pastor, associate pastor(s), committee chairs that most often recruit staff (e.g., Education and Worship), the preschool director, and Focus and Direction members/officers. The secretary/administrative manager should retain a copy for her- or himself.
7. Communicate the essence of the new personnel system to the congregation.

PERSONNEL POLICY DEVELOPMENT AND EMPLOYEE CLASSIFICATION

Policy Development and Distribution

The personnel liaison/personnel committee chair is responsible for overseeing the development, revision, and distribution of church policies.

Any active church officer or committee member can recommend a new policy and procedure or a change to an existing policy and procedure.

The personnel liaison/personnel committee chair is responsible for reviewing policies and procedures at least once during her or his tenure but no longer than every two years to insure policies are consistent with programs, activities, and practices of the church.

By reference, the current personnel policies for the church's denomination are invoked and shall be consistent with these policies.

Policy Responsibility

The pastor, officers, and committee chairs are responsible for policy. The pastor is responsible for overseeing the day-to-day execution of church policy with the assistance of the church staff.

Employee Classifications

I. Non-Ordained Staff

Federal law states that "executive, administrative, professional and outside salesmen" are classified as exempt personnel in *non-church* organizations. A significant segment of the definition states that "exempt" status requires that an employee perform the majority (at least 40%) of her or his time on "management or supervisory duties." All other employees would be classified as nonexempt.

Even though a church's administrative and preschool staff are not subject to federal wage and hour law, it is recommended that churches conform to those laws for employees who would be classified as nonexempt (not exempt from overtime pay). Such a policy will facilitate wage competitiveness with other businesses who recruit from the same labor pool as your church. It will also affirm to the staff and community that your church treats its employees fairly.

Employees of graded K-6 programs at churches are regulated by federal labor and wage and hour laws.

In keeping with the above job classification practice, nonexempt positions would be paid *at least* the federal minimum wage and one and one-half times the employee's hourly wage for all hours worked over 40 hours per week during the pay period in which the hours were actually worked. Hours worked in excess of 40 hours per week may *not* be carried over to the next pay period.

For example, a part-time or full-time bookkeeper or janitor/housekeeper would generally be classified as nonexempt employees under federal wage & hour law.

A. Full Time
    If you do not have a policy, it is suggested that employees who work at least 35 hours per week for six or more months per year be classified as full time and be eligible for the defined church benefit plan (see Employment, Personnel Policy 601.0, on page 64 for a suggested benefit plan guide).

B. Part Time
    If you do not have a policy, it is suggested that employees who work less than 35 hours per week or less than six months per year be classified as part time and be ineligible for the defined church benefit plan except those benefits specifically suggested for part-time employees in Employment, Personnel Policy 601.0, on page 64.

II. Ordained Staff and Selected Nonordained Salaried Staff

Even though such church personnel are not subject to federal wage and hour law, it is suggested that you treat these employees as if they were subject to federal law and therefore classified as exempt (exempt from overtime pay). Utilizing this strategy will enable you to develop salary ranges for each staff position.

The pastor, associate pastor(s), Christian education director, music director, youth director, preschool director, bell choir coordinator, organist and secretary/administrative manager (or similar job titles) would be classified as exempt by federal wage and hour law, due to the nature of their job duties, if they were covered by this law.

Church policy should limit the work week of these positions to a five-day, 50-hour work week (see Working Conditions of Salaried Staff, Personnel Policy 607.0, on page 98).

III. Policies and Procedures

The following policies outline the procedures that pertain to employment at the church. Be sure to check your denomination's directives as they relate to employment, particularly of ordained staff.

Policy Development: See Administration Policy 100.0
Personnel Philosophy: See Personnel Policy 600.0

Employment: See Personnel Policy 601.0
Fair Treatment: See Personnel Policy 602.0
Discipline: See Personnel Policy 603.0
Leave of Absence: See Personnel Policy 604.0
Salary & Performance Evaluation: See Personnel Policy 605.0
Exit Interview: See Personnel Policy 606.0
Working Conditions (Work Week/Salaried Staff): See Personnel
    Policy 607.0
Ordained Staff: See denominational directives

APPENDIX 010

POLICY AND PROCEDURE

SUBJECT: **Policy and Procedure Development**

I. PURPOSE
    To define policy and to establish a system for its responsibility, preparation, approval, and control.
II. POLICY DEFINITION
    A. A policy is a written statement defining the church's position with respect to broad objectives that the officers have approved. Further, it is a long-term directive dealing with matters of church-wide importance. A policy acts as a guide for consistently carrying out goals and actions for the present and future.
    B. Policies are written for two main reasons:
        1. To provide employees with information about the general course of action that the pastor and church officers deem suitable and desirable;
        2. To communicate information about laws, regulations, and other constraints that employees must follow in carrying out their job duties.
III. RESPONSIBILITY FOR POLICY
    The church officers and pastor are responsible for the development of policy.
IV. POLICY DEVELOPMENT
    A. Development begins when an officer, pastor, or other staff member, acting on her or his own initiative or at the suggestion of others, determines the need for revising an existing policy or initiating a new policy.
            The officer or employee recognizing the policy need prepares a draft of what she or he feels should be written in the policy.
    B. If it is determined by church officers and/or the pastor or other staff members that a policy is needed or a change in policy is deemed appropriate, the policy is presented to the church officers and the pastor for approval.
    C. If the policy is approved by the church officers and the pastor, the pastor will sign the policy. If the policy is personnel related, the personnel liaison will also sign the policy, assign a policy number, and post the date officers approved the policy (date effective).
V. NUMBERING SYSTEM
    A. New Policies: The major functional areas of the church are assigned the following numbers for use in the Policy Manual:

Administration	100.0
Budget/Stewardship	200.0
Community Outreach	300.0
Education	400.0

61

Mission	500.0
Personnel	600.0
Property & Maintenance	700.0
Worship	800.0

All policies within a given functional area will be numbered sequentially. A review of the previous highest number will dictate the proper number to be used for a new policy.

B. Revisions or Changes: Revisions or changes will change the number to the right of the decimal of the policy.

EXAMPLE:	Original	100.0
	First Revision	100.1
	Second Revision	100.2

Only the number to the right of the decimal will change; after nine revisions, the revision number will revert back to zero.

VI. RESPONSIBILITY FOR POLICY MANUAL

A. Since the majority of the policies and procedures are personnel related, it shall be the responsibility of the personnel liaison to:
1. Develop or assist in the development of other church policies;
2. At least every two years analyze existing policies, initiate and coordinate appropriate revisions;
3. Serve in an advisory and interpretive capacity on church policy matters;
4. Publish all new policies and procedures and changes to existing policies and distribute to:
   a. Pastor and other ordained staff
   b. Secretary/administrative manager
   c. Focus and Direction members/officers and committee chairs;
5. Educate the above (A.4.), especially new committee chairs, concerning new personnel policies and procedures.

B. It shall be the responsibility of each of the persons named in A.4. above to keep their Policy Manual up-to-date. When a new or revised policy is received, the old policy is to be destroyed and replaced with the new or revised policy.

It is also the responsibility of the above to ensure that church policies are being complied with by all officers, employees and church members.

Approved by	Date Effective	Supersedes	Policy Number
Pastor, Personnel Liaison & Officers		New	100.0

POLICY AND PROCEDURE

Subject: **Personnel Philosophy**

I. PURPOSE
    To convey to the ordained and nonordained staff that we as a church,
    through the personnel committee, with the aid of the personnel liaison, will
    manage our human resources in a manner that results in trust between the
    pastor, officers, congregation, and staff.

II. PERSONNEL COVERED
    All ordained and nonordained personnel.

III. RESPONSIBLE FOR ADMINISTERING
     Pastor and personnel liaison.

IV. POLICY
    We shall treat every individual with concern, dignity, and fairness in terms
    of assigned job duties, working conditions, pay and benefits, and promotion
    consideration.
        In return, we ask that you as an employee perform your jobs to the best
    of your ability and take responsibility for making suggestions to your
    immediate supervisor as to how we can better serve our congregation.

V. PROCEDURE
    If at any time you feel that you are not being treated fairly from an employ-
    ment standpoint you may directly contact the personnel liaison (name and
    phone number) for a confidential, off-premises meeting. See Employee Fair
    Treatment, Policy 602.0.

Approved by	Date Effective	Supersedes	Policy Number
Pastor, Personnel Liaison & Officers		New	600.0

APPENDIX 030

POLICY AND PROCEDURE

Subject: **Employment**

I. PURPOSE
    To insure that the most qualified job applicants are selected for employment, that the church complies with federal and state employment laws, and that employee wage equity is maintained in the church's salary administration plan.

II. PERSONNEL COVERED
    All staff.

III. RESPONSIBLE FOR ADMINISTERING
     Pastor and personnel liaison.

IV. POLICY
    A. NEW POSITIONS: Positions must be approved by the committee with budget responsibility and compensation must be appropriated in the annual budget before any recruitment activity can commence.
    B. PAY: The wage offered for a position must be between the minimum and the midpoint of the salary range for the position to be filled, based on the experience and education of the applicant (see Salary and Performance Evaluation Administration, Policy 605.0).
    C. SUBSTANCE ABUSE OR SEXUAL HARASSMENT: If either prohibited activity is suspected, an investigation will be conducted by the personnel liaison at the request of the pastor.
        Substance abuse is defined as the use of illegal drugs and/or the abuse of legal drugs or alcohol.
        If substance or sexual harassment abuse by an employee is substantiated after investigation, the personnel liaison will make a recommendation to address the situation to the church officers after consulting legal counsel, if appropriate.
        Such abuses by an employee shall be grounds for dismissal.
    D. BENEFIT PLAN
        1. Full Time Employees
            a. *Health Insurance Plan:* A full-time employee may participate in the health insurance plan after three months employment. The church pays the employee cost of plan; family members may be enrolled in the group plan, with the cost paid by the employee.
            b. *Retirement Plan:* After one year of employment, such an employee is eligible to participate in the Church Annuity Plan

with __ percent of salary contributed by the church. The employee may contribute up to __ percent of her or his salary to the Plan.

c. *Vacation:* After one year of employment, full-time employees are eligible for 10 days of paid vacation; after ten years, they are eligible for 15 days paid vacation; and after 20 years, they are eligible for 20 days paid vacation. Since vacation is provided for employee refreshment, vacation may not be carried over to the next year of paid in lieu of vacation.

Unused vacation will be paid at employment separation.

Vacation accrual may be used for an approved leave of absence (see Policy 604.0)

d. *Holidays:* The seven paid holidays each year are New Year's Day, Easter Monday, Memorial Day, Independence Day, Labor Day, Thanksgiving, and Christmas. If a holiday falls on a weekend, the following Monday will be a paid holiday.

e. *Illness, Medical, Dental, and/or Family Leave:* After three months of employment, a full-time employee earns a half-day paid leave each month for personal illness and/or the illness of a son/daughter/spouse/ parent and/or medical/dental visit.

There is no accrual limitation for this leave but the unused accrual will not be paid to the employee upon termination of employment.

2. Part Time Employees

Part-time employees will be paid for the Thanksgiving and Christmas holidays, but only in an amount equal to the hours normally worked per day. They may take one week of vacation without pay after one year of employment and two weeks of vacation without pay after two years employment.

V. PROCEDURE

A. EMPLOYMENT: Applicants for an approved position must complete the appropriate Employment Application form. They are to be interviewed by the appropriate person(s). Employment references must be investigated by the personnel liaison or an appointed member of the personnel committee for at least the past five years of employment history, using the Employment Reference Investigation form and/or the Employment Reference Inquiry form.

B. OFFER LETTER: After the above requirements have been satisfied the designated personnel committee member will prepare an offer letter for the search committee chair's signature. The search committee chair is responsible for signing and mailing *two copies* of the offer letter to the candidate selected for employment. Note that a copy of the offer letter is to be returned by the candidate to the search committee chair, who will give same to the secretary for filing in the employee's personnel file.

C. PERSONNEL ACTION NOTICE: This form is to be use to document *any* employee action (such as employment; paid leave, vacation, or illness; address change; salary increase; leave of absence; termination, etc.).

D. PAY: Nonordained staff are paid *Weekly/Biweekly/Semimonthly/ Bimonthly/Monthly* [choose one]. Ordained staff are paid *Semimonthly/ Bimonthly/Monthly* [choose one].

Approved by	Date Effective	Supersedes	Policy Number
Pastor, Personnel Liaison & Officers		New	601.0

APPENDIX 031

SAMPLE JOB DESCRIPTION

Position: Choir Director   Department: Music
Employee's Name: Date Prepared:
Supervisor's Name: Pastor   Committee Responsible To: Worship

DUTIES
I.   Planning and Coordinating
    1. Act as liaison among members of music staff, pastors, and worship committee.
    2. Attend staff meetings as scheduled.
    3. Plan worship music with music staff and pastors.
    4. Develop and administer the Music Department budget, including approval of all expenditures by music staff.
    5. Monthly, suggest hymns to pastors to support liturgical readings for worship services.

II. Choral Work
    1. Conduct regular and special rehearsals throughout the year.
    2. Recruit and train members of all choirs.
    3. Maintain and expand music library (insuring that music is stamped, sorted and filed).
    4. Select choral music for worship services with input from senior pastor.
    5. Prepare for choir rehearsals by studying music to achieve artistic interpretation.
    6. Provide for own personal and professional development through reading of periodicals and books and by attending workshops.
    7. Mail reminders about choir special event.
    8. Consult with individual choir members before and after rehearsals to encourage and improve their performances.

III. Worship Services
    1. Rehearse with choirs and soloists before worship services.
    2. Direct music portions of all church functions involving music.
    3. Oversee setup of musical components in sanctuary or social hall for all worship services and/or functions, insuring materials and equipment (music, chairs, music stands, and instruments) are available.
    4. Develop congregational participation in music through emphasis on hymn and psalm singing.

IV. Other
    1. Serve as liaison between music program and such activities as retreats, Vacation Bible School, and other special events.
    2. Plan and execute special music programs and/or concerts.

3. Audition and arrange music for soloists and instrumentalists when applicable.
4. Consult with family members regarding music for weddings and funerals as required.
5. Write articles for church community publications to enhance attendance of music programs.
6. Secure substitute organist, pianist, and other musicians as needed.
7. Purchase and maintain musical instruments per annual budget.
8. Secure volunteers to assist with arranging for accompanists, maintaining music library, and leading children's choirs.
9. Receive annual evaluation by senior pastor and worship committee as to effectiveness of music program.
10. Coordinate choir retreats, tours, etc.
11. Evaluate music program to meet changing needs of congregation in the context of church's mission statement.

APPENDIX 032

EMPLOYMENT APPLICATION
(Please Print)

Name: _____   Date: _____
     First   Middle   Last

Present Address: _____ _____
          Street/Box   City   State   Zip   How Long?

Social Security No.: _____   Phone _____

Form of Transportation to be Used if Employed? _____

Contact in case of an emergency: _____ _____
                        Name & Relationship   Phone No.

Education: H.S. Graduate? Y/N   College Graduate? Y/N   Attend School Now? Y/N

Military Service: Dates of Active Duty _____   National Guard? Y/N

Previous Employment: **(Please begin with the most recent, including present)**

Employer's Name _____   Position _____
Address _____   Phone _____
Dates of Employment _____   Supervisor _____
Pay: $_____ Week/Month Reason for Leaving _____

Employer's Name _____   Position _____
Address _____   Phone _____
Dates of Employment _____   Supervisor _____
Pay: $_____ Week/Month Reason for Leaving _____

(Use the back of this application to list any other employers)

Fair Credit Reporting Act Disclosure: In making this application it is acknowledged that we may request information regarding your character, employment, and background. Upon written request, information concerning the above will be obtained. False or incomplete information in this application is grounds for termination of employment consideration or employment, if already employed.

I CERTIFY THAT THE ABOVE INFORMATION IS ACCURATE AND COMPLETE:

_____

Signature

An Equal Opportunity Employer

69

APPENDIX 033

EMPLOYMENT APPLICATION SUPPLEMENT
Nonordained Staff

Name: _____

Education (continued): If college or technical school graduate, note Degree/Diploma.

_____

College/Technical School   City   Degree/Diploma

Professional Registration(s): _____

Interests & Hobby(s): _____

SELF DESCRIPTION

1. Please write a brief description of yourself: _____

_____

_____

2. What are your goals? **Professional:** _____

_____

Personal: _____

_____

3.   What did you accomplish in your present or past employment(s)? _____

_____

4,   Describe your most significant work-related accomplishment during the past

twelve months: _____

_____

5.   How do others view your business strength(s)? _____

_____

6.   How do others view your business "need for improvement" attribute(s)? _____

_____

7.   To what to do you attribute your business success? _____

_____

Signature: _____   Date: _____

_____

TO BE COMPLETED BY CHURCH IF EMPLOYMENT OFFER MADE

Reporting Date: _____   Position_____   Salary $_____   By_____

EMPLOYMENT REFERENCE INVESTIGATION
(phone)

Applicant: _____ Soc. Sec. No. _____

Co./Institution Contacted: _____ Person/Dept.: _____

Phone No.: _____ Date: _____ By: _____

Conclusion (Favorable or Unfavorable): _____

QUESTIONS

1. Dates of Employment? _____

2. Position at Separation? _____

3. Salary at Separation? _____

4. Work-Related Strengths? _____
_____
_____

5. Need for Improvement Areas/Weaknesses? _____
_____
_____

6. Leadership Ability/Potential? _____
_____

7. Relationship with Subordinates? _____
_____

8. Relationship with Supervisor? _____
_____

9. Attitude towards Position and Company? _____
_____

10. Overall Work Performance Evaluation During Past Year (Based on Performance Evaluations)? _____

11. Eligibility for rehire?: Eligible Ineligible (Circle One). If "Ineligible" please state reason
_____

12. Other Questions/Comments? _____
_____

EMPLOYMENT REFERENCE INQUIRY

Church Name
Street Address/Box No.
City/State/Zip
FAX No.

The below former employee, by signing this form, has given you permission to answer the following questions candidly:

Former Employee _____   _____
                         Given/Maiden Name(s)   Signature

Social Security No. _____   Date: _____

1. Dates of Employment: _____

2. Position at Separation: _____

3. Salary at Separation: _____

4. Overall Work Performance Evaluation During Last Year of Employment: _____
_____
_____

5. Eligibility for reemployment: Eligible   Ineligible   (Circle one).
If "Ineligible" please state reason (Please Use Back of Form if Needed): _____
_____
_____

_____
Supervisor's Name (Please Print)

_____   _____
Company/Institution   Address

APPENDIX 036

SAMPLE EMPLOYMENT OFFER LETTER

Mrs. Brenda Cope
0000 Walnut St.
Anytown, VA., 22980

September 1, 1999

Dear Brenda:

On behalf of the search committee, officers, congregation, and pastor of Stone Church, this letter will confirm the verbal offer I made you to become our book-keeper. This position reports directly to Jean, our administrative manager. Our search committee will serve in an advisory role to you during your first year of employment.

Your employment will commence on October 1, 1999.

Your beginning salary with us will be $9.00 per hour for 20 hours per week. You will receive your first performance evaluation in June 2000, and every six months thereafter, by Jean, and a performance evaluation with salary consideration in December 2000.

You are eligible for 10 days unpaid vacation per year with the dates for same predetermined with Bruce, the pastor. Vacation may be requested for a two-week period or may be taken in one week increments.

You will receive two paid holidays, which are Thanksgiving and Christmas.

We are all excited about your becoming a *vital* part of our ministry at Stone Church! Please sign and return one copy of this offer letter in the enclosed, self-addressed envelope while retaining the other copy for yourself. If you have a further questions, please call me.

In Christ's Service,

Erwin Berry, Chair, Search Committee

I understand and accept the above conditions of employment,

_____   _____

Signature   Date

Copies: Pastor Bruce
         Personnel File of Brenda Cope
         Personnel Liaison

73

APPENDIX 037

FEDERAL IMMIGRATION (I-9) FORM

U.S. Department of Justice
Immigration and Naturalization Service

OMB No. 1115-0136
Employment Eligibility Verification

INSTRUCTIONS
PLEASE READ ALL INSTRUCTIONS CAREFULLY BEFORE COMPLETING THIS FORM.

Anti-Discrimination Notice. It is illegal to discriminate against any individual (other than an alien not authorized to work in the U.S.) in hiring, discharging, or recruiting or referring for a fee because of that individual's national origin or citizenship status. It is illegal to discriminate against work eligible individuals. Employers **CANNOT** specify which document(s) they will accept from an employee. The refusal to hire an individual because of a future expiration date may also constitute illegal discrimination.

Section 1 - Employee. All employees, citizens and noncitizens, hired after November 6, 1986, must complete Section 1 of this form at the time of hire, which is the actual beginning of employment. **The employer is responsible for ensuring that Section 1 is timely and properly completed.**

Preparer/Translator Certification. The Preparer/Translator Certification must be completed if Section 1 is prepared by a person other than the employee. A preparer/translator may be used only when the employee is unable to complete Section 1 on his/her own. However, the employee must still sign Section 1 personally.

Section 2 - Employer. For the purpose of completing this form, the term "employer" includes those recruiters and referrers for a fee who are agricultural associations, agricultural employers, or farm labor contractors.

Employers must complete Section 2 by examining evidence of identity and employment eligibility within three (3) business days of the date employment begins. If employees are authorized to work, but are unable to present the required document(s) within three business days, they must present a receipt for the application of the document(s) within three business days and the actual document(s) within ninety (90) days. However, if employers hire individuals for a duration of less than three business days, Section 2 must be completed at the time employment begins. **Employers must record: 1)** document title; **2)** issuing authority; **3)** document number, **4)** expiration date, if any; and **5)** the date employment begins. Employers must sign and date the certification. Employees must present original documents. Employers may, but are not required to, photocopy the document(s) presented. These photocopies may only be used for the verification process and must be retained with the I-9. **However, employers are still responsible for completing the** I-9.

Section 3 - Updating and Reverification. Employers must complete Section 3 when updating and/or reverifying the I-9. Employers must reverify employment eligibility of their employees on or before the expiration date recorded in Section 1. Employers **CANNOT** specify which document(s) they will accept from an employee.

- If an employee's name has changed at the time this form is being updated/ reverified, complete Block A.

- If an employee is rehired within three (3) years of the date this form was originally completed and the employee is still eligible to be employed on the same basis as previously indicated on this form (updating), complete Block B and the signature block.

- If an employee is rehired within three (3) years of the date this form was originally completed and the employee's work authorization has expired **or** if a current employee's work authorization is about to expire (reverification), complete Block B and:
  - examine any document that reflects that the employee is authorized to work in the U.S. (see List A or C),
  - record the document title, document number and expiration date (if any) in Block C, and
  - complete the signature block.

Photocopying and Retaining Form I-9. A blank I-9 may be reproduced provided both sides are copied. The Instructions must be available to all employees completing this form. Employers must retain completed I-9s for three (3) years after the date of hire **or** one (1) year after the date employment ends, whichever is later.

For more detailed information, you may refer to the INS Handbook for Employers, (Form M-274). You may obtain the handbook at your local INS office.

Privacy Act Notice. The authority for collecting this information is the Immigration Reform and Control Act of 1986, Pub. L. 99-603 (8 U.S.C. 1324a).

This information is for employers to verify the eligibility of individuals for employment to preclude the unlawful hiring, or recruiting or referring for a fee, of aliens who are not authorized to work in the United States.

This information will be used by employers as a record of their basis for determining eligibility of an employee to work in the United States. The form will be kept by the employer and made available for inspection by officials of the U.S. Immigration and Naturalization Service, the Department of Labor, and the Office of Special Counsel for Immigration Related Unfair Employment Practices.

Submission of the information required in this form is voluntary. However, an individual may not begin employment unless this form is completed since employers are subject to civil or criminal penalties if they do not comply with the Immigration Reform and Control Act of 1986.

Reporting Burden. We try to create forms and instructions that are accurate, can be easily understood, and which impose the least possible burden on you to provide us with information. Often this is difficult because some immigration laws are very complex. Accordingly, the reporting burden for this collection of information is computed as follows: **1)** learning about this form, 5 minutes; **2)** completing the form, 5 minutes; and **3)** assembling and filing (recordkeeping) the form, 5 minutes, for an average of 15 minutes per response. If you have comments regarding the accuracy of this burden estimate, or suggestions for making this form simpler, you can write to both the Immigration and Naturalization Service, 425 I Street, N.W., Room 5304, Washington, D. C. 20536; and the Office of Management and Budget, Paperwork Reduction Project, OMB No. 1115-0136, Washington, D.C. 20503.

Form I-9 (Rev. 11-21-91) N

EMPLOYERS MUST RETAIN COMPLETED I-9
PLEASE DO NOT MAIL COMPLETED I-9 TO INS

U.S. Department of Justice
Immigration and Naturalization Service

OMB No. 1115-0136
Employment Eligibility Verification

Please read instructions carefully before completing this form. The instructions must be available during completion of this form. **ANTI-DISCRIMINATION NOTICE.** It is illegal to discriminate against work eligible individuals. Employers CANNOT specify which document(s) they will accept from an employee. The refusal to hire an individual because of a future expiration date may also constitute illegal discrimination.

Section 1. Employee Information and Verification. To be completed and signed by employee at the time employment begins

Print Name: Last	First	Middle Initial	Maiden Name
Address (Street Name and Number)		Apt. #	Date of Birth (month/day/year)
City	State	Zip Code	Social Security #

I am aware that federal law provides for imprisonment and/or fines for false statements or use of false documents in connection with the completion of this form.	I attest, under penalty of perjury, that I am (check one of the following): A citizen or national of the United States A Lawful Permanent Resident (Alien # A_____ An alien authorized to work until___/___/___ (Alien # or Admission #_____

Employee's Signature	Date (month/day/year)

Preparer and/or Translator Certification. *(To be completed and signed if Section 1 is prepared by a person other than the employee.) I attest, under penalty of perjury, that I have assisted in the completion of this form and that to the best of my knowledge the information is true and correct.*

Preparer's/Translator's Signature	Print Name
Address (Street Name and Number, City, State, Zip Code)	Date (month/day/year)

Section 2. Employer Review and Verification. To be completed and signed by employer. **Examine one document from List A OR** examine one document from List B **and** one from List C as listed on the reverse of this form and record the title, number and expiration date, if any, of the document(s)

List A	OR	List B	AND	List C
Document title: _____		_____		_____
Issuing authority: _____		_____		_____
Document #: _____		_____		_____
Expiration Date (if any): __/__/__		__/__/__		__/__/__
Document #: _____				
Expiration Date (if any): __/__/__				

CERTIFICATION - I attest, under penalty of perjury, that I have examined the document(s) presented by the above-named employee, that the above-listed document(s) appear to be genuine and to relate to the employee named, that the employee began employment on *(month/day/year)* ___/___/___and that to the best of my knowledge the employee is eligible to work in the United States. (State employment agencies may omit the date the employee began employment).

Signature of Employer or Authorized Representative	Print Name	Title
Business or Organization Name	Address (Street Name and Number, City, State, Zip Code)	Date (month/day/year)

Section 3. Updating and Reverification. To be completed and signed by employer

A. New Name (if applicable)	B. Date of rehire (month/day/year) (if applicable)

C. If employee's previous grant of work authorization has expired, provide the information below for the document that establishes current employment eligibility.

Document   Title:_____Document   #:_____Expiration   Date   (if   any):__/__/__

I attest, under penalty of perjury, that to the best of my knowledge, this employee is eligible to work in the United States, and if the employee presented document(s), the document(s) I have examined appear to be genuine and to relate to the individual.

Signature of Employer or Authorized Representative	Date (month/day/year)

Form I-9 (Rev. 11-21-91) N

APPENDIX 038

PERSONNEL ACTION NOTICE

NEW EMPLOYEE or **EMPLOYEE DATA** or	1) Name: Last, First & Middle	2) Social Secty. No.	3) Effective Date/Mo.-Day-Yr.	4) Home Phone No.
	5) Street Address or Box No.	6) City	7) State 8) Zip Code	9) Birth Date

	10) Employment Date	11) Job Title	12) Salary Grade	13A) Job Classification:
				     Non-Ordained ( )
				     Ordained ( )

WAGE CHANGE	13B) Job Classification:
	    Full Time ( )
	    Part Time ( )
	    Seasonal ( )
		14A) Wage:
		    To $
		
		    From -$
		
		14B) Paid Wkly ( )
		    Bi-Weekly ( )
		    Monthly ( )
		    Bi-Month.( )
		    Semi-Mo. ( )
			15A) Next Perf.
			    Eval. Date:
			
			15B) Next Wage
			    ReviewDate:
				EEOC REQUIRED DATA
				16A) Caucasian ( )
				    African Amer. ( )
				    Oriental ( )
				    Spanish ( )
				    Amer. Indian ( )
				    Other_____ ( )
				16B) Female ( )
				    Male ( )
				16C) Single ( )
				    Married ( )

JOB STATUS CHANGE	17A) Classification ( )
	    Job Title ( )
	    Promotion ( )
	    Demotion ( )
	    Other_____
		17B) To
		
		    From
			18A) Ordained ( )
			    Non-Ord ( )
			18B) Full Time( )
			    Part Time( )
			    Seasonal ( )
				19) Salary Grade:
				    To
				
				    From

ABSENCE	20A) Leave: Paid Vacation
	    Non-Paid Vacation
	    Paid Family
	    Non-Paid Family
	    Paid Illness
	    Non-Paid Illness
		20B) Lv of Abs
		    Illness/Dis ( )
		    Maternity ( )
		    Military ( )
		    Other _____
			20C) Funeral Leave
			    Paid
			    Non-Paid
				21) Dates:
				    From
				
				    To

TERMINATION	22) Voluntary ( )
	    Involuntary ( )
	    Reduction in
	    Staff ( )
		23) Last Day
		    Worked:
			24A) Severance
			    Pay: Yes ( )
			    No ( )
				24B) No. of Days/
				    Dollar Amount:

APPROVAL/ COMMENTS	25) Sr. Pastor _____ Date_____
	    Supervisor _____ Date_____
	    Personnel Liaison/
	      Committee Chair_____ Date_____
	    Officer _____ Date_____
			26) Comments:	

76

APPENDIX 039

EMPLOYEE ORIENTATION PROCEDURE

Employment Information:

Position: _____

Employment Date: _____

Starting Salary: _____

Work Schedule_____

First Perf. Eval. Date: _____

Social Security No_____

Work/Alien Permit # (if applicable): _____

Orientation Record:
1. Greeted by supervisor
2. Completed Employment forms:
   a. W-4: Federal and State
   b. I-9: Department of Immigration
   c. State Work Permit for minors
   d. Employment application (if not completed)
   e. Insurance applications (if eligible)
3. Tour of church and work area; introduction to coworkers and review of work schedule
4. Explain church rules (working from the Employee Manual with employee)
   a. Three-month training period
   b. Importance of attendance and punctuality
   c. Phone supervisor when ill or delayed
   d. Parking
   e. Personal appearance
5. Performance evaluations and wage increases
6. Staff meeting: day and time and importance of attending

7. Explain Fair Treatment policy for dealing with concerns
8. Other information/Answer questions
9. Work Safety and Fire Prevention:
   a. Contact supervisor in case of accident
   b. Location of first aid kit
   c. Slippery floors
   d. Objects on floor
   e. Lifting objects
   f. Proper shoes (Housekeeping employees)
10. On the job training:
    a. Review of work materials and schedule
    b. Review of job description
    c. Introduction to trainer who will explain job
    d. Employee observes job tasks
    e. Employee performs job tasks
    f. Trainer corrects employee if needed
11. End of day review with employee by supervisor
    a. How did your day go?
    b. Questions?

Orientation completed

_____ _____ _____
Date   Supervisor   Employee

APPENDIX 040

POLICY AND PROCEDURE

SUBJECT: **Employee Fair Treatment**

I. PURPOSE
    To insure that employees are treated fairly in terms of employment matters.

II PERSONNEL COVERED
    All employees.

III. RESPONSIBILITY FOR ADMINISTERING
     Pastor and personnel liaison.

IV. POLICY-PROCEDURE
    An employee who feels she or he has not been treated fairly in terms of employment, pay, or working conditions and who is unable to resolve the concern with her or his immediate supervisor may speak with the individual designated as the personnel liaison between the church's administration committee and the church staff.

    An employee is encouraged first to attempt to resolve the concern or problem with her or his immediate supervisor or the pastor before contacting the personnel liaison.

    Employees have the assurance of the church that all employee concerns will be resolved in the best interest of the employee and the church and that no disciplinary action will be taken against an employee for voicing her/his concern.

Approved by	Date Effective	Supersedes	Policy Number
Pastor, Personnel Liaison & Officers		New	602.0

APPENDIX 050

POLICY AND PROCEDURE

SUBJECT: **Employee Discipline**

I. PURPOSE
    To insure that employees are treated fairly regarding discipline undertaken
    to correct undesirable work performance.

II. PERSONNEL COVERED
    Nonordained Staff.

III. RESPONSIBILITY FOR ADMINISTERING
    Pastor and personnel liaison.

IV. POLICY
    A. Employees with three or more months of employment may not be
        terminated unless:
        1. At least one written notice has been given on the appropriate
            performance evaluation form for a similar or different offense in
            the preceding 12-month period that would be cause for termination
            of employment.
        2. The employee has been given a reasonable time period to correct
            the deficiency (see V.C. below).
        3. At least one level of supervision above the offending employee has
            approved the termination on the performance evaluation form.

V. PROCEDURE
    A. *Written warning:* An oral warning is usually given to an offender prior
        to giving a written warning.
    B. *Examples of situations justifying written warning notices:*
        1. A performance evaluation overall rating of "Marginal" or "Unsatis-
            factory."
        2. Unauthorized or unexcused absenteeism.
        3. Repeated tardiness.
        4. Violation of work or safety rules.
        5. Improper member relations or sexual harassment.
    C. *Documenting a Performance Deficiency:* When a situation justifies a
        written warning, the action must be documented. The performance
        evaluation form is to be used for a formal warning.
            The written warning should set forth in detail the reason for the
        warning, together with the corrective action the employee must take. A
        time limit of one to three months (or a reasonable time period to enable
        the employee to correct the deficiency or improve her or his perfor-

mance) for corrective action must be noted on the evaluation form. The written warning must be reviewed with the employee, and the employee should sign it or a notation should be made by the supervisor that the warning was read to the employee and she or he refused to sign it.

D. *Administering a Warning:* An oral or written warning should always be done in private.

E. *Suspension for Fact Finding:* Normally, employees who commit or who are suspected of committing any of the violations listed in VI.E. below should be suspended for a period not to exceed three days, during which time a full investigation of the circumstances is to be made. The employee must be advised at the time of suspension that the investigation will be conducted and that she or he will be advised within three days of the decision reached. All facts must be obtained and reviewed with the pastor and personnel liaison for approval prior to making the final decision. When a decision has been reached, the employee must be advised of the decision in person.

F. *Suspension for Discipline:* Suspension of an employee from work is a serious penalty and should be imposed only in extreme situations. Gross insubordination or an instance in which an employee commits or is suspected of committing a serious violation of church policy are examples of instances that may justify suspension of one to three days maximum until a decision is reached concerning termination. See Section VI.E. below for additional reasons warranting suspension for disciplinary action.

G. *Distribution of a Warning:* A copy of the warning must be given to the offending employee; the supervisor retains a copy and a copy is placed in the employee's personnel file.

VI. INVOLUNTARY TERMINATION

Because of the unsettling impact that a discharge without notice has on an employee and the job security of all personnel in general, it is vitally important that such discharges be administered with fairness and in good taste. A discharge without notice should take place only after careful review of all the facts and only after approval of the pastor, personnel liaison, and church officers.

A. *Less than Three Months Employment:* All employees are considered to be in a "training" status during the first three months of employment. During this time, performance and suitability for a position are to be carefully evaluated. At any time during the first three months of employment an employee may be terminated without written notice if the facts support the action.

A supervisor must receive approval of a termination from his or her immediate supervisor during the first three months of employment via a completed Personnel Action Notice. Employees terminated during the first three months of employment will not receive severance pay or any other benefit accrual payout.

B. *Three Months or More Employment:* All employees with three or more months employment must be given a written warning prior to termination as explained in V.C. above.

C. *Permanent Reduction in Workforce:* An employee terminated because of a permanent reduction in membership or a church restructuring that permanently eliminates her or his position shall be considered to have terminated because of reduction in force. Employees terminated due to reduction in force shall be separated on the basis of job performance. Seniority will be considered when performance has been determined to be equal.

D. *Health Insurance:* A full-time employee's health insurance coverage will continue through the end of the month in which the employee is separated from the church.

Such employees may continue to be enrolled in the company's health insurance plan by law (C.O.B.R.A.) for 18 months (24 months beginning on January 1, 2000) after separation provided the employee pays the entire cost of the insurance to the payroll department by the first of every month.

E. *Reasons for Termination without Notice:* The following violations will result in termination without warning, advance notice, and/or severance pay:

- Willful damage or gross negligence to church property.
- Possession of a weapon on church premises.
- Drinking, intoxication, or possession of alcoholic beverages on the job.
- Being under the influence of narcotics, use of narcotics, or possession or solicitation of narcotics for use while at work, other than prescription drugs as prescribed by a physician.
- Gambling on church premises.
- Absence without authorization for three or more work days (consecutive or otherwise) during any 12 consecutive months.
- Disclosure of confidential or sensitive church information.
- Assaulting or fighting with another employee or member on church property, on or off duty.
- Conviction of a felony or serious misdemeanor.
- Willful falsification of church records, such as an employment application, payroll information, or financial or insurance records.
- Absence from work beyond the period for which a leave of absence has been granted by the church.

- Taking other unauthorized employment while on a leave of absence.
- Theft of church property.
- Willful violation of church policy.

VII. VOLUNTARY RESIGNATION

A. *Employee Notice to Company:* A nonordained employee is expected to give notice of at least two weeks in advance of employment termination.

The choir director is expected to give notice at least four weeks in advance of employment termination.

An ordained employee is expected to give notice of at least eight weeks in advance of employment termination.

Approved by	Date Effective	Supersedes	Policy Number
Pastor, Personnel Liaison & Officers		New	603.0

APPENDIX 060

POLICY AND PROCEDURE

SUBJECT: **Employee Leave of Absence**

I. PURPOSE
To insure consistency and fairness in the administration of employee leave of absences.

II. PERSONNEL COVERED
Full-time nonordained and ordained staff.

III. RESPONSIBLE FOR ADMINISTERING
Pastor and personnel liaison.

IV. POLICY
Eligible employees may be placed on leave of absence with the understanding that the employee intends to return to work for the church at the conclusion of the leave of absence.

A leave of absence for longer than three months precludes the church from assuring the employee that she or he may return to the position held at the time the leave of absence began.

However, should a leave of absence continue beyond a three-month period, every effort will be made to employ the employee in any position opening for which she or he is qualified.

An employee not returning to work the day following the conclusion of an approved leave of absence will be terminated from employment.

A. *Types of Leave of Absences:*
   1. Personal: An absence of up to one month as approved by the pastor, supervisor, and the personnel liaison.
   2. Medical and Family: An absence of up to three months as approved by the pastor, supervisor, and the personnel liaison. Such leave may be authorized for a seriously ill employee (Medical leave) or to care for a child or parent who is seriously ill (Family leave).
   3. Parental: An absence of up to six weeks as approved by the pastor, supervisor, and the personnel liaison. Such leave may be authorized for the birth, adoption, or guardianship of a child by an employee.
   4. Military: Absences of two weeks for National Guard summer camp or for an extended period of time for National Guard or Reserve members in the event of a national emergency as declared by the president.

B. *Wages and Benefits:*
   1. Wages
      As approved by the pastor or the supervisor of an employee and by the personnel liaison, full-time nonordained and ordained employees employed before the effective date of this policy receive one half-day of leave per month, with accrual retroactive to their date of employment and with a maximum of six weeks accrual for personal, medical and family, parental, and/or military leave of absences.

      Full-time nonordained and ordained employees employed after the effective date of the policy accrue one half-day of leave per month after three months of employment to a maximum of six weeks accrual for personal, medical and family, parental, and/or military leave of absences.

      Note: Employees not covered by a Disability Income insurance plan accrue one half-day per month after three months employment for an indefinite time period for disability purposes only. The definition of "disability" would be the same as the definition used by the state Workers Compensation Law.

      Regular wages will not be paid during a leave of absence nor will vacation leave accrue during a leave of absence.
   2. Benefits
      The church will pay the premiums of all benefits of eligible employees during an approved leave of absence.

      Eligible employees may also utilize their vacation leave accrual during a leave of absence if needed.

      There shall be no break in employment service with regard to length of service recognition during an approved leave of absence but any salary increases approved by the officers will be prorated by the number of months the employee is on leave.
C. *Employment with another Church/Company during a Leave of Absence:* Under no circumstance may an employee be employed by another organization while on a leave of absence. Such a violation of policy will result in termination of employment.

V. PROCEDURE
In the event of a medical, family, or parental leave of absence the employee is required to provide her or his supervisor with a written statement from her or his doctor as to the reason for the leave of absence request and a projected date for returning to work.

A Personnel Change Notice form should be completed by the pastor or supervisor of the employee to be placed on the leave of absence and given to the personnel liaison for her or his approval PRIOR to communicating approval of such leave to the employee.

It is the responsibility of the employee on leave to contact her or his supervisor in writing to request reinstatement of employment with the anticipated date of return to work. In the event of a medical, family, or parental leave, the employee's doctor is required to provide her or his supervisor with a written statement indicating a date when the employee may safely resume work.

Approved by	Date Effective	Supersedes	Policy Number
Pastor, Personnel Liaison & Officers		New	604.0

APPENDIX 070

<h2 style="text-align:center">POLICY AND PROCEDURE</h2>

SUBJECT: **Salary and Performance Evaluation Administration**

I. PURPOSE
    To pay ordained and nonordained staff competitively, fairly, consistently, and equitably, recognizing that such a process will enable our church to attract, motivate, and retain personnel.

II. PERSONNEL COVERED
    All.

III. RESPONSIBLE FOR ADMINISTERING
    Pastor, personnel liaison, and secretary/administrative manager/personnel coordinator.

IV. POLICY
    The church is committed to achieving the purpose stated above by paying employees a competitive wage. Employees are to be appraised by their supervisor annually with salary consideration, unless the employee's salary exceeds the maximum of her or his salary range, and six months later for performance only. SALARY INCREASES ARE AWARDED ONLY IF PERFORMANCE IS EVALUATED AS "GOOD" OR BETTER.
    Should a salary exceed the maximum of an individual's salary range a salary review will not be given until a salary survey taken by the personnel liaison reveals that the maximum of the salary range be increased, resulting in the salary of the individual affected being below the maximum of the salary range, or the individual is promoted to a higher salary range.
    This policy also provides that an employee with a salary below the minimum of a salary range to be reviewed every six months with salary consideration until she or he reaches the minimum of the salary range. SALARY INCREASES ARE AWARDED ONLY IF PERFORMANCE IS EVALUATED AS "GOOD" OR BETTER.
    Employees in Salary Grade(s) _____ will receive a salary review three months after employment, nine months later and annually thereafter.
    Employees are to be appraised objectively, accurately, and fairly at the times prescribed by this policy and the church approved Performance Evaluation forms shall be used.

<h3 style="text-align:center">Performance Evaluation System</h3>

The performance evaluation process is the cornerstone of the church's salary award system. Every employee is entitled to know how she or he is performing as judged by their immediate supervisor. Different evaluation forms are utilized, as outlined below, to insure that an employee understands how she or he is performing.

Performance Evaluation Forms:
1. "Nonordained Staff"—for all hourly and salary nonordained personnel.
2. "Ordained Staff"—for all salaried ordained personnel.
3. "Nonordained and Ordained Staff"—for selected personnel working with goals.

Performance Definitions:
Once a supervisor has evaluated an employee on each position factor and/or goal, the supervisor determines the "Overall Evaluation" of an employee.

1. **Outstanding (O):** Performance is substantially higher than required. This individual consistently makes superior contributions to the organization and requires minimal supervision. (This evaluation category will be added two-three years after this policy becomes effective to enable those administering performance evaluations to gain experience with the process.)

    Such an employee may be awarded a salary increase before the scheduled salary review date if the following guidelines are met. Early awards will receive close scrutiny and are for exemplary performance only if:
    a. At least six months have elapsed since the last salary award.
    b. The next scheduled salary review is no more than six months away.
    c. Performance is clearly "Outstanding" as defined above.
    d. Making the award will not create a salary inequity among other church personnel.
    e. The salary increase is approved by the senior pastor, the immediate supervisor recommending the increase, and the personnel liaison.
2. **Excellent (E):** Performance is consistently above the position's requirements and is marked by initiative and high quantity and quality of work. The employee's judgment is sound and position knowledge is superior to most other employees in this position.
3. **Good (G):** Performance meets the position requirements. Such employees may be capable of achieving an "Excellent" evaluation or may not be capable of better performance.
4. **Marginal (M):** An employee is performing some position duties satisfactorily and others unsatisfactorily. A "Marginal" overall evaluation denotes performance deficiency and may constitute a first written warning.

    Such an evaluation requires that the employee be appraised again in 30, 60, or 90 days (depending on the time required to rectify the performance deficiency and as determined fair by the supervisor and/or the pastor). If, at the time of the second appraisal, performance has improved, the employee may be awarded a salary increase within the "Good" salary guidelines. Such a salary award recycles the next performance-salary review date. If, at the time of the second appraisal, performance has not improved, the evaluation constitutes a second warning and could result in termination of employment.

5. **Unsatisfactory (U)**: The overall performance of an employee is judged to be below the requirements for the position and is unacceptable. Prior oral and/or written notice of "Unsatisfactory" performance may have been given to the employee. Prior to initiating termination action, the pastor and/or the employee's immediate supervisor must obtain the approval of the personnel liaison (see Discipline, Policy 603.0).

6. **Too Early To Rate (T)**: An employee has not been in her or his position long enough to evaluate her or his performance fairly.

Salary Awards:

As stated earlier, employees are reviewed annually with salary consideration, with increases to be effective January first of each year (or the first day of a new fiscal year), except those employees noted in the Salary Review Frequency section of this policy. Employees who have not been employed 12 months but more than six months will receive a prorated wage/salary increase for the number of months employed.

Salary increases are based on the following conditions:

1. Overall job performance as indicated on the Performance Evaluation form for a given position (this is the primary determinant).
2. Position of employee's salary within her or his salary range.
3. Date and amount of the last salary award.
4. Salaries of peers, subordinates, and supervisors.
5. Salaries of comparable positions.
6. Church's financial condition.

Salary increase amounts consistent with the church's budget are determined each calendar year by the personnel liaison.

Promotional Salary Awards:

Salary increases are given when an employee advances to a position of greater responsibility. In determining the amount of salary increase, a supervisor should consider the readiness of the employee to accept full responsibility for the new position, fairness of present salary in the new salary range, and the date and amount of any previous salary increase.

A promotional salary award may be 5 percent to 10 percent as determined by the above criteria and as approved by the personnel liaison. The only exception is when a promotion increase does not raise the salary to the minimum of the salary range for the new position, the employee will receive salary increases every six months until her or his salary exceeds the minimum salary of the new salary range.

Salary Adjustments:
Salary adjustments may be granted for the following exceptional situations:
1. *Internal Salary Inequity:* The personnel liaison determines that a salary inequity exists and the inequity cannot be corrected through the salary review process. The administration committee must approve any action to correct a salary inequity and will notify the pastor of their recommendation.
2. *External Salary Inequity:* If the administrative committee, which is responsible for salary administration, determines that an employee's salary is significantly lower than another church's salary for a comparable position and the salary review process will not correct the inequity, a recommendation will be communicated to the pastor.
3. *Salary below Position's Salary Range:* In such cases the employee's salary will be reviewed every six months until her or his salary reaches the minimum of the salary range.
4. *Demotion in Position:* When a demotion is deemed appropriate, the salary should be reduced by the amount of salary increase received at the time of promotion or an amount reflective of the position demoted to but that will not result in financial hardship for the employee. The demoted employee should receive a scheduled salary review at his or her next annual salary review. However, the demoted employee's salary will be governed by the salary range of her or his new position.

Salary Review Frequency:
1. Employees below the minimum of a salary range are to be reviewed every six months until they reach the minimum of the salary range.
2. Employees paid above the minimum but below the maximum of a salary range are to be reviewed annually until they reach the maximum of their salary range.
3. Employees paid at or over the maximum of a salary range are ineligible for salary increases until their salary range is revised upwards and their salary is under the maximum of their salary range.

Salary Ranges:
Each position will have a Salary Range with a minimum, midpoint and a maximum.
Minimum: New employment applicants should be hired at the minimum of the salary range for her or his position. However, an experienced applicant may be employed at a salary above the minimum but below the midpoint for a position. An employee may not be hired above the midpoint

except for an exceptional situation. Such a situation must have approval of the personnel liaison.

Midpoint: This point in a salary range can be utilized as a gauge in determining if an experienced, competent employee is being paid fairly and competitively.

Maximum: The maximum amount of salary that may be paid for a position.

Review of Compensation:

A salary and benefit survey is to be undertaken annually by the personnel liaison to determine the market value of each church position. Survey sources such as Christian Ministry Resources, State Employment Security Commission, denominational data, and salary and benefit data from local churches may be collected.

Salary Analysis:

Individual salaries will be reviewed at least annually by the personnel liaison to insure salary equity among all personnel.

V. PROCEDURE

Step 1: Each November the secretary/personnel coordinator will give the pastor and other supervisors the appropriate performance evaluation forms for each subordinate to be evaluated.

Step 2: Also in November, all supervisors complete performance evaluations for their subordinates and review them with the pastor. The pastor also completes performance evaluations for each of her or his subordinates. Officers give input to the pastor for her or his use in evaluating the ordained staff.

Step 3: Each December, the pastor will present completed staff performance evaluations to the personnel liaison along with recommended pay increases.

Step 4: The original evaluation forms are returned to the pastor and supervisors, who review them with subordinates. The officers will prepare an evaluation of the pastor, which is presented by the Focus and Direction Task Force. A copy of the performance evaluation form is given to the employee at the time of appraisal review.

Step 5: Copies of the evaluation forms are placed in the employee's personnel record file. Personnel Action Notices are completed by the secretary for employees to receive salary/wage increases and forwarded to the bookkeeper.

Approved by	Date Effective	Supersedes	Policy Number
Pastor, Personnel Liaison & Officers		New	605.0

SAMPLE JOB PERFORMANCE GOALS

Pastor:
1. Visit or contact prospective church members who have attended at least two activities (worship service; Wednesday evening function; etc.).
   - Goal: Increase church membership (currently ___) by ___ percent this year.
2. Teach Sr. High Bible study twice monthly.
   - Goal: Increase participation (currently ___) of Sr. High students in church and Sunday school activities by ___ percent this year.

Christian Education Director:
1. Direct Christian Education classes and church youth activities.
   - Goal: Increase Sunday School attendance (currently ___) by ___ percent this year.
2. Direct Sunday School teacher recruitment and curriculum development.
   - Goal: All teacher positions filled and curricula for all classes in place by September 1.
3. Personally teach Jr. High Bible study class twice each month.
   - Goal: Increase Jr. High student attendance (currently ___) by ___ percent this year.

Choir Director:
1. Direct Chancel Choir, Jr. & Sr. High Choir, two youth choirs, organist, and two hand bell choirs.
   - Goal: Complete annual plan for each of the above groups by December 1.
2. Assist Preschool Director with music presentations during worship service by preschool students at least twice during the school year.
   - Goal: Increase preschool enrollment (currently ___) by ___ percent this year.

Preschool Director:
1. Preschool students present at least two music presentations during worship service while school in session.
   - Goal: Increase preschool enrollment (currently ___) by ___ percent this year.

Secretary:
1. Direct Sr. Housekeeper/Custodian in the performance of her or his job duties. Meet with Sr. Housekeeper/Custodian at least weekly following pastor's staff meeting to review church activities scheduled for that week. Tour church and Education buildings with Sr. Housekeeper/Custodian and offer suggestions on improving cleanliness and orderliness of buildings and assisting members responsible for functions.
   - Goal: No complaints from officers or members regarding cleanliness or orderliness.

APPENDIX 072

PERFORMANCE EVALUATION AND IMPROVEMENT PLAN
Nonordained Staff

Employee: _____ Position: _____

Overall Rating: ( ) Outstanding   ( ) Excellent   ( ) Good
               ( ) Too Early to Rate   ( ) Marginal   ( ) Unsatisfactory

Evaluator: _____ Evaluation Date: _____
                                    Next Evaluation Date: _____

Performance Factor	O	E	G	T	M	U	Improvement Plan/Comments
Personal Appearance							
Attendance							
Attitude Towards Position							
Working Relationship with Others							
Working Relationship with Supervisor							
Knowledge of Job							
Quality of Work							
Quantity of Work							
Initiative							
Problem Solving							
Cost Control							
Effective Use of Time							
Other							

Personal Development Goals: _____

_____

APPENDIX 073

PERFORMANCE EVALUATION AND IMPROVEMENT PLAN
Ordained Staff

Employee: _____ Position: _____

Overall Rating: ( ) Outstanding   ( ) Excellent   ( ) Good
               ( ) Too Early to Rate   ( ) Marginal   ( ) Unsatisfactory

Evaluator: _____ Evaluation Date: _____
                                        Next Evaluation Date: _____

Performance Factors	O	E	G	T	M	U	Comments
Attitude Towards Responsibilities							
Working Relationship with Staff and Volunteers							
Working Relationship with Congregation							
Job Knowledge-Skills (Preaching; teaching; pastorate; administration; coordination; management)							
Increased Growth (Member spirituality, participation and membership)							
Increased Member Giving (Pledges-other)							
Responsive to Congregation Needs							
Communication with Congregation, Staff & Officers							
Direction of Staff and Volunteers							

Performance Factors	O	E	G	T	M	U	Comments
Judgment							
Community Involvement							
Personal Development							

Goals:

_____

_____

_____

APPENDIX 074

PERFORMANCE EVALUATION & IMPROVEMENT PLAN
Ordained and Nonordained Staff

Employee: _____ Position: _____

Overall Rating: ( ) Outstanding   ( ) Excellent ( ) Good
            ( ) Too Early to Rate ( ) Marginal ( ) Unsatisfactory

Evaluator: _____ Evaluation Date: _____
            Next Evaluation Date: _____

Performance Goals	O	E	G	T	M	U	Comments

PERFORMANCE NARRATIVE (Overall performance since previous Evaluation):

_____

_____

_____

_____

_____

_____

_____

_____

_____

_____   _____
Employee's Signature   Date

_____

SALARY AWARD

Annual Salary Evaluation or Promotion? (Please Circle)

_____   _____
Current Salary   Date of Last Award

_____   _____   _____
Salary Award Recmd.   Salary Approved   Award Effective Date

Approvals:

_____   _____   _____
Pastor/Date   Officer/Date   Personnel Liaison/Date

Instructions:

1. Complete Evaluation form. If applicable, complete above salary data.
2. If Evaluation w/ salary award obtain Personnel Liaison's approval **PRIOR** to conducting Evaluation.
3. Conduct Evaluation w/ employee, have employee sign Evaluation & give copy to employee.
4. Return original Evaluation to Secretary/Administration Manager for filing in employee's Personnel file.

APPENDIX 080

POLICY AND PROCEDURE

SUBJECT: **Employee Exit Interview**

I. PURPOSE
To aid the personnel committee in determining and correcting causes of employee turnover and to insure that employees are treated fairly regarding employment matters.

II. PERSONNEL COVERED
Ordained and Nonordained staff.

III. RESPONSIBLE FOR ADMINISTERING
Personnel Liaison.

IV. POLICY
Ordained and nonordained staff resigning from the church are to be interviewed by the personnel liaison within three days after the resignation has been given to the employee's immediate supervisor.

An exit interview is normally not required for an employee terminated for cause. However, if an exit interview is deemed appropriate by the personnel liaison and pastor, an exit interview may be conducted.

V. PROCEDURE
A Personnel Action Notice (PAN) is completed by the immediate supervisor for an employee who has either resigned voluntarily or has been terminated for cause.

A copy of the PAN is forwarded to the bookkeeper and a copy is placed in the employee's personnel file.

The personnel liaison prepares a written report of the exit interview findings within one week following the interview. Prior to the final typing of the report, the interviewer will review the exit interview findings with the immediate supervisor of the interviewee and with the pastor to insure that the information given is factual from the perspective of the immediate supervisor.

After the above step is completed, the exit interview report is typed by the personnel liaison and distributed to the pastor. A copy of the report will be placed in the employee's personnel file.

Approved by	Date Effective	Supersedes	Policy Number
Pastor, Personnel Liaison & Officers		New	606.0

APPENDIX 090

POLICY AND PROCEDURE

Subject: **Working Conditions of Salaried Staff**

I. PURPOSE
    To insure that the salaried staff are treated fairly in terms of their working conditions.

II. PERSONNEL COVERED
    Salaried staff.

III. RESPONSIBLE FOR ADMINISTERING
    Officers and personnel liaison

IV. POLICY
    The approved work week for the salaried staff is 50 hours, with two days off each week.
        An ordained staff member is not expected to work more than three evenings during a work week.

V. PROCEDURE
    Should a pattern emerge that indicates a salaried staff member is working in excess of 50 hours per week for one or more months, the individual concerned should begin to maintain a record for one month. The record would then be given to the personnel liaison, who would in turn give the record to the appropriate church officer.
        The affected individual would meet with the personnel liaison and church officer and scrutinize the individual's job duties in an attempt to reassign duties that would not compromise the mission of church but would enable the individual to work within the 50-hour work week.

Approved by	Date Effective	Supersedes	Policy Number
Pastor, Personnel Liaison & Officers		New	607.0

APPENDIX 100

ANNUAL OFFICER SURVEY OF SERVICE EXPERIENCE

Please place an **X** on the line that most closely represents your experience as an officer and place in the secretary's mailbox <u>within one week of receipt</u>. The survey results will be published within one month after all responses have been received. Thank you for your faithfulness by participating in this important survey.

I served as a _____.

My initial orientation/training as an officer was helpful & adequate.

Agree ____ ____ ____ ____ ____ ____ ____ Disagree

My role was clearly defined & explained.

Agree ____ ____ ____ ____ ____ ____ ____ Disagree

The church staff was available and helpful to me.

Agree ____ ____ ____ ____ ____ ____ ____ Disagree

Comments/motions I made during our meetings were received openly by the pastor/moderator and were given adequate consideration.

Agree ____ ____ ____ ____ ____ ____ ____ Disagree

I feel that I contributed to the decision making process of our body.

Agree ____ ____ ____ ____ ____ ____ ____ Disagree

I generally support the actions taken by our officers and feel the pastor/moderator was effective in leading our body.

Agree ____ ____ ____ ____ ____ ____ ____ Disagree

The decisions of the officers have generally had a positive impact on our church.

Agree ____ ____ ____ ____ ____ ____ ____ Disagree

My faith has been strengthened by having served as an officer.

Agree ____ ____ ____ ____ ____ ____ ____ Disagree

My overall experience as an officer has been positive.

Agree ____ ____ ____ ____ ____ ____ ____ Disagree

NOTE COMMENTS ON REVERSE SIDE OF SURVEY IF NEEDED.

Date Survey Completed: _____

ANNUAL COMMITTEE SURVEY OF SERVICE EXPERIENCE

Please place an **X** on the line that most closely represents your experience as a committee member and place in the secretary's mailbox within <u>one week after of receipt</u>. The results of the survey will be published within one month after the responses have been received. Thank you for your faithfulness and participation in this important survey.

I served on the _____ Committee.

Our committee is necessary and its purpose/function is clear to me.

Agree ____ ____ ____ ____ ____ ____ ____ Disagree

The comments/motions I made during our meetings were received openly and were given adequate consideration by the committee.

Agree ____ ____ ____ ____ ____ ____ ____ Disagree

The committee has generally functioned effectively and efficiently.

Agree ____ ____ ____ ____ ____ ____ ____ Disagree

I feel that I contributed to the decision-making process of our committee.

Agree ____ ____ ____ ____ ____ ____ ____ Disagree

Our chair has effectively directed the efforts of our committee.

Agree ____ ____ ____ ____ ____ ____ ____ Disagree

Our committee has made a positive contribution to the life of our church.

Agree ____ ____ ____ ____ ____ ____ ____ Disagree

The church staff was available and helpful to our committee.

Agree ____ ____ ____ ____ ____ ____ ____ Disagree

My overall experience as a member of this committee has been positive.

Agree ____ ____ ____ ____ ____ ____ ____ Disagree

To improve the effectiveness of this committee I would suggest (print your suggestion(s) below and on the back of the Survey if more space is needed):

Date Survey Completed: _____

EMPLOYEE HANDBOOK

(Church Name, Address & Phone No.)

We're pleased that you are considering or have been selected for employment with our church!

Congratulations and welcome to our church. We wish you every success in your employment with us and promise you that we will do our part in assisting you in meeting your personal goals.

You have been or may be selected to join our staff of professionals, who are committed to excellence in serving our Lord and the congregation of our church.

Your future and ours is determined by the manner in which we satisfy every member and potential member each day.

Regardless of your position, you are important in helping us meet our objectives, but we also want you to enjoy your work with us. At times you may be asked to do a task that is not in your job description to better serve our church. We appreciate your understanding of this need.

Our commitment to you: We shall treat you fairly with regard to your job security, salary, benefit program, and job advancement opportunities.

We are proud to have you associate your good name with ours!

> In Christ's Service,
> Pastor

CHURCH HERITAGE

(Insert a brief history of your church and a statement about its mission.)

PERSONNEL PHILOSOPHY

As a church we are committed to treating you as an employee with respect, dignity, and Christian love and trust that you will wholeheartedly support the pastor and staff in service to our congregation and our Lord.

EMPLOYMENT INFORMATION

I. JOB STATUS
    A. **Full Time:** An employee who works 35 hours or more per week for six or more months in succession.
    B. **Part Time:** An employee who works less than 35 hours per week or 35 hours or more per week for less than six months in succession.

C. **Temporary:** An employee who works less than six months at any given time.

D. **Training Status:** The first three months of employment.

II. WORK SCHEDULES

The work schedule discussed with you during your employment interview will be covered again during your first workday orientation.

We schedule exactly the number of employees required to meet our work load. If one employee is late or doesn't show up for work, the others have to do not only their jobs but also that of the missing employee. The result is that some task may not get done and our congregation suffers. You are a valued member of our staff!

When the need arises you may be asked to work beyond your scheduled time or do other tasks requiring completion.

WHAT YOU CAN EXPECT FROM OUR CHURCH

I. PAY

You will be paid every other Friday for the previous two weeks or the portion of the previous two weeks you worked.

You may not be paid in advance of regular pay days.

II. RECORDING TIME WORKED

You will be expected to note on the time card for a pay period (10 work days) the exact time you begin work and the exact time you stop work each day. The secretary/administrative manager responsible for approving payroll will explain where your time card is kept. If your supervisor asked you to work beyond your scheduled time, she or he will initial your time card for that day. You will be paid one and one-half times your regular wage for hours worked beyond 40 hours in a work week.

III. WAGE DEDUCTIONS

The law requires that we deduct social security (F.I.C.A.) and federal and state withholding taxes based on the number of dependents you claimed on your W-4 forms. By January 31 of each year you will receive your W-2 form, which will reflect your total earnings and taxes withheld for federal and state taxes during the previous year.

IV. PERFORMANCE EVALUATIONS

Your supervisor will review your work performance based on the following performance factors after three months employment, and each June and December thereafter.

Wage Consideration: Your supervisor will inform you when you will be reviewed with wage consideration.

Performance Evaluation Factors and/or Goals: The following performance factors apply to nonordained staff: Personal Appearance; Attendance; Attitude toward Position; Working Relationship with Others; Working Relationship with Supervisor; Knowledge of Job Duties; Quality of Work; Quantity of Work; Initiative; Problem-Solving Ability; Cost Control; Effective Use of Time; Goals; and Other.

You will also be evaluated on the achievement of the goals for your position that you and your supervisor agreed upon at the beginning of the year.

Your overall evaluation ("Outstanding," "Excellent," "Good," "Marginal," "Unsatisfactory," or "Too Early to Rate") will determine the amount of your wage increase and your job advancement progression within the church.

Employees receiving an overall performance evaluation of "Marginal" or "Unsatisfactory" will not receive a wage increase and will be reviewed again in one to three months to determine their employment and wage status (see Job Performance Warning below).

Training Period: Your first three months of employment are designated as your training period. If during this period your performance is evaluated by your supervisor as "Unsatisfactory," you may be terminated without written warning. However, your supervisor will warn you orally when she or he detects that there is a job performance problem.

Your supervisor will assist you in becoming proficient in your new job. If you have a job or personal problem, feel free to discuss it with your supervisor.

When you have been employed for three months and have received a performance evaluation of "Good" or better, you will be removed from training status.

Job Performance Warning: If at any time after three months of employment (the training period) but prior to a scheduled performance evaluation, your supervisor determines that your job performance is "Unsatisfactory" or "Marginal," your supervisor will give you a formal, written warning that will become a part of your personnel file.

Your supervisor will determine a probationary period of one to three months. At the end of the probation period your supervisor will again review your job performance and if you are evaluated as "Good" or better, you will be removed from probation status. If your performance is evaluated as "Unsatisfactory" or "Marginal" a second time, you may be terminated depending on the nature of your job deficiency.

We seldom have situations requiring disciplinary action and when such situations occur, your supervisor will do everything possible to help you overcome your performance deficiency.

Resolving Your Concerns: Our Fair Treatment Policy is that every employee will be treated fairly in matters of pay, benefits, promotions, working conditions, and the resolution of employment-related concerns. If you have a concern discuss it with your immediate supervisor. If your concern is not resolved to your satisfaction by your immediate supervisor, you may speak with the pastor or meet confidentially with the personnel liaison.

V. CAREER ADVANCEMENT

We shall always consider our employees for position openings before recruiting outside the church.

Career Advancement Ladder

The career ladder below shows how you can progress within our church. *(List the highest paid nonordained position from your salary ranges and then the next highest paid position and so on.)*

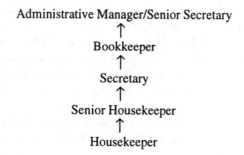

Administrative Manager/Senior Secretary
↑
Bookkeeper
↑
Secretary
↑
Senior Housekeeper
↑
Housekeeper

VI. EMPLOYMENT RECOGNITION

All employee will be recognized for their years of service to the church on their first and fifth anniversaries and on every five-year anniversary thereafter.

VII. LEAVE OF ABSENCE

Full-time employees employed three or more months may apply for a leave of absence for personal, medical and family, parental, and military-related reasons only.

Eligible employees may be placed on leave of absence with the understanding that the employee intends to return to work for the church at the conclusion of the leave of absence.

A leave of absence for longer than three months precludes the church from assuring the employee that she or he may return to the position held at the time the leave of absence began.

However, should a leave of absence continue beyond a three-month period, every effort will be made to employ the employee in any position opening for which she or he is qualified.

An employee not returning to work the day following the conclusion of an approved leave of absence will be terminated from employment.

A. **Personal**

An absence of up to one month as approved by the pastor, supervisor, and the personnel liaison.

B. **Medical and Family**

An absence of up to three months as approved by the pastor, supervisor, and the personnel liaison. Such leave may be authorized for a seriously ill employee (Medical leave) or to care for a child or parent who is seriously ill (Family leave).

C. **Parental**

An absence of up to six weeks as approved by the pastor, supervisor, and the personnel liaison. Such leave may be authorized for the birth, adoption, or guardianship of a child by an employee.

D. **Military**

Absences of two weeks for National Guard summer camp or for an extended period of time for National Guard or Reserve members in the event of a national emergency as declared by the president.

VIII. BENEFIT PLAN

A. Full-Time Employees

Federal Social Security (FICA): We match the mandated contribution you make to your federal retirement plan.

Health Care Insurance: After three months of employment, we shall pay the cost for employee-only coverage. You may elect to enroll your dependent(s) at our group rate at your own expense. A payroll deduction will be made for this coverage the first of each month.

Retirement: After one year of employment, we shall contribute __ percent of your wage to a retirement plan. You can personally contribute up to __ percent of your wage with monthly payroll deductions. At least once a year you will receive a statement of earnings for your account.

Vacation: After one year of employment, 10 days of paid leave per year; after 10 years of employment, 15 days of paid leave per year; and after 20 years of employment, 20 days of paid leave per year. Pay will not be given in lieu of vacation leave accrual. Employees may carry over unused leave accrual may not be carried over to another calendar/fiscal year. When warranted, church officers may consider approval of carrying over vacation leave accrual to the following calendar/fiscal year on an exception basis.

Holidays: The seven paid holidays are New Year's Day, Easter Monday, Memorial Day, the Fourth of July, Labor Day, Thanksgiving

Day, and Christmas Day. If a holiday falls on a weekend, the following Monday will be a paid holiday.

Personal, Medical and Family, Parental, and Military Leave: After three months of employment you will earn one half-day per month with unlimited accrual.

Workers' Compensation Insurance: In the unlikely event of a work-related injury, it is essential that you inform your supervisor at once so that prompt medical attention can be obtained for you. State workers compensation pays a portion of your regular wage while you are unable to work as well as most of your medical expenses related to the injury during your recovery.

B. Part Time Employees

Federal Social Security (FICA): We match the mandated contribution you make to your federal retirement plan.

Workers' Compensation Insurance: In the unlikely event of a work-related injury, it is essential that you inform your supervisor at once so that prompt medical attention can be obtained for you. State workers compensation pays a portion of your regular wage while you are unable to work as well as most of your medical expenses related to the injury during your recovery.

Holidays: Thanksgiving and Christmas Days. You will be paid for the number of hours you normally work.

Vacation: After one year of employment, 5 days of unpaid vacation leave will be available for your use. After two years of employment, 10 days of unpaid vacation leave will be available for your use each year.

WHAT WE EXPECT OF YOU

IX. WORK RULES

A. Sexual Harassment: and Substance Abuse

Harassment, including sexual advances, jokes, or comments of any kind, is prohibited. An employee found guilty of such acts will be terminated. You may contact the pastor or the personnel liaison if you are being harassed by another employee.

Substance abuse is defined as the use of illegal drugs and/or the abuse of legal drugs or alcohol.

If abuse in either case is suspected, an investigation will be conducted by the personnel liaison at the request of the pastor. If substance abuse or sexual harassment by an employee is substantiated after investigation, the personnel liaison will make a recommendation to address the situation to the church officers after consulting legal counsel, if appropriate.

B. Personal Appearance

Employees are expected to dress in an appropriate and professional manner and to be bathed and neatly groomed. The pastor or personnel liaison may call the employee's attention to any dress or grooming not deemed appropriate. Their decisions are final and any further dress or grooming in that style could lead to disciplinary action.

C. Smoking

Our church is a smoke-free environment. If you smoke, you may smoke only outside the building and away from all entrances.

D. Telephone and Off-Duty Visitation

Please discourage your friends and relatives from telephoning or visiting while you are working. When you go off duty, don't linger in the work area, keeping your coworkers from getting their jobs done.

We recognize that there will be times when it is necessary for you to be phoned at work and only ask that you keep your conversation short, since we have a limited number of phone lines coming into the church.

E. Causes for Employee Termination without Formal Warning

The below is offered for your protection and to give the church the legal grounds for taking action against an employee who could prove dangerous to your well being.

1. Willful damage or gross negligence to church property.
2. Possession of a weapon on church premises.
3. Drinking, intoxication, or possession of alcoholic beverages on the job.
4. Being under the influence of narcotics, use of narcotics, or possession or solicitation of narcotics for use while at work, other than prescription drugs as prescribed by a physician.
5. Gambling on church premises.
6. Absence without authorization for three or more work days (consecutive or otherwise) during any 12 consecutive months.
7. Disclosure of confidential or sensitive church information.
8. Assaulting or fighting with another employee or member on church property, on or off duty.
9. Conviction of a felony or serious misdemeanor.
10. Willful falsification of church records, such as an employment application, payroll information, or financial or insurance records.
11. Absence from work beyond the period for which a leave of absence has been granted by the church.
12. Taking other unauthorized employment while on a leave of absence.
13. Theft of church property.
14. Willful violation of church policy.

F. Solicitation

Employees may not solicit monies or distribute literature of any kind on church property at any time. The only exception to this policy is in connection with the United Way annual donation drive.

G. Business Expense Reporting

You will be reimbursed for approved church-related business expenses. When making a purchase greater than $25, it is necessary to obtain a purchase order number or approval from the secretary/administration manager or pastor. Please complete the business expense reimbursement form and submit it to the secretary/administrative manager for reimbursement.

H. Work Safety

1. Report any accident by any employee or church visitor to your supervisor.
2. Do not operate any machine unless you have received instructions as to how to use it.
3. Be careful not to lift objects too heavy for you. Get help!
4. Wet floors can cause serious accidents.
   a. Wipe up any spill at once.
   b. When a floor section is wet, SLOW DOWN.
   c. Pick up any object on a floor surface, except glass. Glass should be swept into a dust pan and placed in the trash.
5. Watch where you are walking.
6. Use a ladder—not a box or chair—to reach items in high places.

Please read, sign, and tear out the Employee Handbook Acknowledgment on the last page of this Handbook and give to the person who is to conduct your orientation. The acknowledgment will be filed in your personnel folder.

Again, we are pleased you have chosen to become a part of our dedicated staff! Your supervisor will begin your formal orientation and training on your first day of employment with us . . . WELCOME!!

EMPLOYEE HANDBOOK ACKNOWLEDGMENT

The Employee Handbook has been written to highlight the Personnel Policies and Procedures of our church so that you will understand what we expect of you as an employee as well as what you can expect from us as an employer. Should you desire to read the Personnel Policies and Procedures in their entirety, ask the secretary/administrative manager for the Personnel Policy and Procedure Manual. The Personnel Policy and Procedure Manual may not be taken from the office for any reason.

This Handbook is not intended to serve as an employment contract between you, the church, and its employees. As it becomes necessary to change any of the policies and procedures or benefits described in this Handbook, you will be informed of any such changes.

If you have a question(s) about any of the information in this Handbook, please ask the secretary, the pastor, or your supervisor.

I acknowledge that I have received, read, and understand the contents of the Employee Handbook.

_____

Employee's Name (Please Print)

_____

Employee's Signature

_____

Date

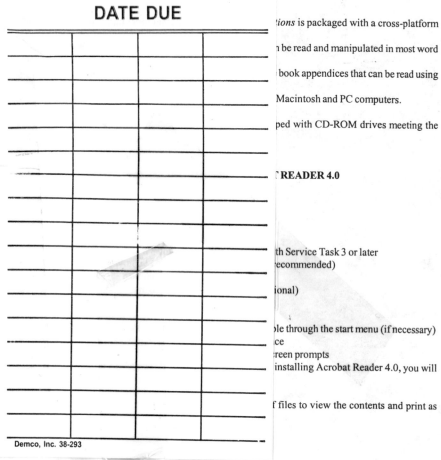

DATE DUE

Demco, Inc. 38-293

tions is packaged with a cross-platform

1 be read and manipulated in most word

book appendices that can be read using

Macintosh and PC computers.

ped with CD-ROM drives meeting the

' READER 4.0

th Service Task 3 or later
ecommended)

ional)

)le through the start menu (if necessary)
ce
reen prompts
installing Acrobat Reader 4.0, you will

f files to view the contents and print as

System Requirements:
- ♦ Apple Power Macintosh computer
- ♦ Apple System Software version 7.1.2 or later
- ♦ 4.5 MB of RAM available to Acrobat Reader (6.5 MB recommended)
- ♦ 8 MB of available hard disk space
- ♦ Additional 50 MB of hard disk space for Asian Fonts (optional)

Installing and uninstalling:
- ♦ Uninstall Acrobat Reader 3.x if desired.
- ♦ Make sure you have at least 10 MB of available disk space
- ♦ Double-click on the Acrobat Reader 4.0 installer and follow the screen prompts

After installation is complete, double-click on any of the .pdf files to view the contents and print as desired.